Basic Python In Finance

Bob Mather

2

FREE GIFT

If you're interested in learning how artificial intelligence will take over your world in the next decade, or you're just trying to get automation tools for your office and business, you will love my book titled 'Artificial Intelligence for Business' below:

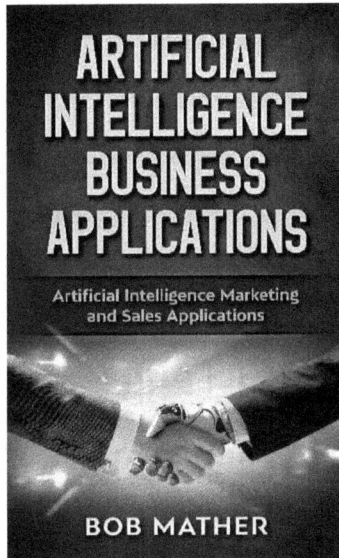

https://bobmatheraibusiness.gr8.com/

Table of Contents

5

Why Python In Finance?

We live in a world where technology has taken root in everything; by everything, we mean literally *everything*. From waking up and to look at your phone to making coffee using your coffee machine, the last decade has seen more inventions and advancements in technology than any other era in human history. Researchers estimate that by 2030, the world will have flying cars to reduce congestion. Amazing, right? And in the excitement of new automation, we have not left business and finance behind, as companies have been turning to technology to stay ahead of their competitors.

In the world of finance, technology is an asset. Technology significantly improves time and efficiency of a business. Companies no longer depend entirely on the financial aspects but look toward new innovations. Technology not only brings out modernization, but it also speeds up the rate of financial transactions and gives out large volumes of data. It will not be wrong to say that technology has become the main distinguisher between institutions.

Programming languages such as R, C+, C++, Java, and Python dominate the game, and this book will cover about everything you need to know about Python in finance. It will cover the following topics among others:

- An introduction to Python and the basics that you will require to get started. Get to know about how to use Python in finance and the benefits that it brings to the table.

- You will learn about the basic trading strategies and time series. Get to know about stock and bonds.

- Time series data and common financial analyses that you will encounter such as volatility calculations, cumulative daily rate of return, moving windows and the dividend calculations among others.

- The common trading strategies that are involved in Python.

This book is mainly aimed at financial professionals and stock investors who wish to get started implementing Python code to automate their finances. It touches on the different areas and their specific codes. Just like Python is an asset to finance, this book is also an asset to you.

Why Python in Finance?

Before we kick everything off and get to the complex parts, we will first begin with examining why Python in finance is important. One reason that makes Python a popular programming language is because it is simple to write, thus making it an excellent tool for traders, analysts, and researchers. A 2018 report by HackerRank 2018 Developer Skills Report showed that the number of financial institutions that were using Python had tripled in the previous two years, i.e. 2016 and 2017. The following are the reasons entrepreneurs are turning to Python for their financial needs.

It is flexible and simple

As mentioned above, Python is easy to understand and deploy. This makes it a perfect tool for handling and dealing with complex financial applications. It is highly accurate and thus reduces the rate of error; a very critical factor in finance, especially when dealing with highly regulated industries. Python is fast, which is a bonus because organizations can build on their software quickly and bring them to the market in no time.

It is rich in tools and libraries

Python has an advantage in that developers need not build tools from scratch. On top of saving the organization tons of cash, it also goes a long way in reducing the time spent on a single development project. If your company's products require integration with third parties, Python has you covered. In short, **it makes everything easier.** Its vast libraries and collections of tools enhance Python's speed, helping to build a competitive structure for organizations seeking to address the needs of consumers that are changing every day by releasing unique products fast enough.

Python is popular

The community behind the development of Python comprises passionate and vibrant developers who have contributed to creating practical tools and organizing many events to share the knowledge and benefits of Python. Each year, the community grows and the number of people opting to use Python is constantly increasing. Experienced developers join the Python community and add to its value, adding to its popularity. Organizations that have invested in Python are certain that technology is here to stay, and there are no signs of it being obsolete anytime in the coming future.

Enables organizations to build their MVPs quickly

Financial organizations need a technology that is scalable and flexible; they need something that will respond quickly to their customers' demands and offer personalized services that will add value to them. Python offers nothing short of this. Python enables developers to create an MVP that will help the organization find a market for their products in no time. The MVP is flawless, and the organization can change or add new codes to suit their products or create new unique ones.

Python bridges data science and economics

Other programming languages like Matlab are less popular with economists who have opted for Python in making their economic calculations. Python's practicality and simplicity in creating formulas and algorithms makes it a prodigy in the game, as Python makes bridging data science and economics simpler than it is.

This is just the tip of the iceberg for why Python is great for finance, and there are still many more reasons you should consider this programming language. One thing for sure is that Python is a giant in the game; moreover, it is simple to write and a great starting point for beginners.

Before going deeper into the various trading strategies, it is essential that we get hold of the basics at first. This book will give you a detailed explanation of Python basics that will go a long way in assisting you to get started. It is essential that you know the basics for Pandas, and have learned your way around NumPy, packages, and Python lists. If you don't know the basics right now, worry not; we've got you sorted.

Chapter Summary

This chapter covered why Python in finance is a great innovation. We went over how financial institutions and data analysts should have a basic knowledge of Python, and we highlighted some other reasons to consider Python.

In the next chapter, you will learn about basic trading strategies and how to invest in various stock assets.

Basic Trading Strategies and Time Series

This chapter will introduce you to various trading strategies using Python. You will also learn business trading using stocks and about time series data.

Financial institutions use Python to make it easier to trade financial **securities** like **bonds, stocks**, and tangible products such as gold and oil.

Before we dive into stock trading and time series data, we want to make sure you understand some basics of finance. If you are a well versed financial professional, you may skip this section.

What Are Stocks and Stock Trading?

Stocks

Stocks are equity investments of a particular corporation, and they represent part of ownership of that corporation. When you buy stocks of a corporation, you become a shareholder in that company, which entitles you to receive that corporation's earnings and assets.

The **shareholders** receive profits from the proceeds of the company in the form of **dividends**. If you buy ordinary or common stocks, you will have voting rights at the annual meetings of that company, but there is no guarantee that you will receive dividends. Shareholders who buy **preferred stocks** have no voting rights, but that guarantees they receive dividends from the company proceeds.

In finance, a stock is a **financial security** that represents ownership in terms of shares to a company. The company issues shares at a particular amount; this amount determines your claim on the company's assets and its performance.

Companies raise funds for engaging in their projects through shares to the public. Investors interested in such stocks buy them, thus providing the capital needed for the company.

Investors buy and sell stocks through **brokers** or **online trade**. Before buying any stocks, make sure you evaluate the different stocks to know which is suitable for you. You should also decide how many you need to purchase.

Bonds

When a company raises money through issuing debt or borrowing a loan from a banking institution, they receive *bonds* instead of *stock*. A **bond** is a fixed income instrument representing a loan issued to a **borrower** by the **investor**.

Companies, states, and other sovereign governments use bonds to finance major projects or grow their business. Governments also use bonds when borrowing money. **Debtholders**, or **creditors**, issue these bonds.

Large organizations need more money that average banks can give; therefore, bonds provide a solution to those organizations by allowing several individual investors to assume the role of a **lender**.

Stock Trading

Stock trading involves buying and selling *existing* or *previously issued* stocks. Depending on the company's performance, the share prices can be high or low. Stock prices fluctuate based on the current market price or based on **supply and demand** in the share market.

Traders buy stocks of the company at low prices with anticipation that the prices will rise, allowing them to sell the stocks at higher prices later.

Some traders may use a **short-selling trading strategy**, similar to the concept just described. This strategy is when the trader borrows shares from the company and sells immediately, hoping to buy them later at a lower price, then return the borrowed shares to the lender. In return, traders can realize more profit.

Investment banks and **stock exchange institutions** develop various trading strategies and frameworks to help them make investment decisions. Python is one of the most popular programming languages used to develop and design these trading strategies.

Similar to building a project, developing trading strategies contains a series of steps: from planning the strategy to designing and testing the performance of this strategy.

These trading strategies are used to test historical data based on the rules defined with the strategy before being applied in the real market. Testing will help determine how effective is your strategy and areas you need to improve.

Trading Strategies

The best trading strategy is the **price action strategy**, which will give you the best return on investment. **Forex traders** rely on a variety of trading strategies to determine the best time to invest in stocks and when to sell them. Investors innovate new **trading patterns** and **analytical methods** to make it easier to understand price market movements.

Most investors use a **day trading pattern**, where they buy and sell financial instruments within one day or even have multiple transactions in a single day.

Be careful if you want to use a **day trading strategy**, especially if you are new. The transaction costs and risks with this strategy are very high. Choose the best trading strategy that limits your losses and find a reliable **broker** that will help you trade successfully.

If you rely on **online brokers**, make sure they have an advanced platform that shows real-time streaming of **stock quotes** and **advanced charting tools**. These applications will enable you to modify multiple orders in quick succession.

Basic Principles for Successful Trading strategy

Have the latest stock market news

Knowledge is power, and having knowledge of the latest stock market news and other events will help you succeed. Do a lot of research and inform yourself about the current economic outlook of the country and **interest rate plans**.

Keep a list of the stocks you would like to trade on and the companies to buy these stocks. Read business news from various financial websites to learn the happenings of the general market.

Put aside some funds.

Once you keep a list of stocks to trade, you also have to decide how much you're willing to risk trading. Always set some funds aside which you can use to trade and also prepare yourself for possibly losing them. Trading is a win-lose strategy; you can either win or lose your money.

Set a trading time

Set aside some time for you to use for trading each day. You need time to track the markets and spot opportunities that arise during the **trading hours**. If you're using a day trading strategy, grabbing an open opportunity quickly is the key.

Start small

If you're new in the stock market, starting small is the way to go. You can focus on a maximum of two stocks per go, which makes it easy to track and find opportunities. You can also trade in fractional shares where you can invest in smaller amounts. For example, if a company is trading at $250, you can buy shares worth $50 (one-fifth of a share) from the brokers.

Keep away from penny stocks

Always avoid buying stocks selling at low prices because most of the time these stocks are illiquid and can become delisted from the major stock exchange companies. Most trade these stocks over-the-counter, which means you can easily lose your investment.

Be realistic

When trading, be realistic about the strategy. Not every strategy you win will be profitable; many traders win 50% to 60% of all their trades. Take a limited risk with each trade and define your **entry** and **exit methods** for each trade.

Stick to the plan

To succeed, you need to develop a trading strategy in advance and always stick to it. This will help you move fast and be successful. Your plan will help evaluate your trade closely and avoid chasing profits.

Strategies

Follow the Trend

This means you buy shares when the prices rise and short sell when the price drops. You buy shares with the assumption that the rising and falling of share prices will continue to do so.

Scalping Strategy

In this strategy, a speculator will exploit a small price gap created by the **bid-ask spread**. It allows you to enter and exit the market within a short timeframe.

Contrarian Investment

In the contrarian approach, you buy stocks during their fall in price and short sell during the price rise. Investors operate on the assumption that the rising price will reverse and then drop after a while.

Trending News

This strategy allows investors to buy stocks when there is good news and short sell when there is bad news on the stocks. One has to be careful when using this strategy, as it can lead to both higher profits and losses.

There are pros and cons to all of the above strategies. Do what suits your level of involvement and risk to make it work for you.

Time Series Data

This is a series of data points taken at a particular time interval. In stocks, a time series tracks the changing prices of shares over a specified time period, and it forecasts stock prices over a specified period.

VIX Validation vs. Prediction

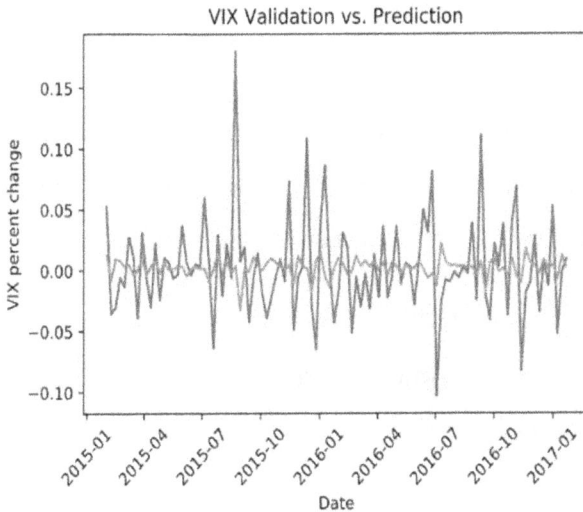

We would usually plot **time series data** via **line charts** and use them in forecasting data trends. Investors carry out a time **series analysis** on time series data to extract meaningful statistics and obtain other characteristics of data. Time series data predicts *future* data values based on the *previously recorded* data values.

The data recorded can be on an annual, quarterly, monthly, weekly, daily, or hourly basis. The investor analyses the data and draws a chart depicting the sequence of observations.

Analysing time series data is a step-by-step preparation process. Beyond analysing future values, it also helps develop a meaningful and accurate forecast of the recorded data.

A **time series chart** is a series of snapshots or events that have taken place at a regular time interval. It is an ideal tool for investors to determine stock trends in the market before investments.

The chart acts as a dashboard or data visualization tool that shows data points at successive time intervals. All data points show the prices and time to measure. The dashboard allows investors to spot trading patterns easily and analyse how the stock market prices are changing.

Importing Time Series Data in Python

We store time series data in the form of a **.csv file**, or a spreadsheet format. The data comprises two columns: the *dates* and the *values*.

We can import this data into a Python program using **Pandas library**. Pandas time series package can easily integrate with any data set and has specific time series data structures for dealing with dates and times. A **timestamp** represents a single point in time. To create a timestamp from strings with a different date/time format, we would use the _to_datetime()_ function.

Here is how we would import Pandas and convert a date to a timestamp:

```
import Pandas as pd
pd.to_datatime('2019-09-27 3:45pm')
```

Output

```
Timestamp('2019-09-27 15:45:00')
```

Example 2

```
import Pandas as pd
pd.to_datetime('25/8/2019')
output
Timestamp('2019-25-08 00:00:00')
```

The *to_datetime()* function tells Pandas to convert to the date/time format based on the input provided. Pandas function automatically converts date/time to **month/day/year**.

pd.to_datetime('25/8/2019') converts to *Timestamp('2019-25-08 00:00:00')*

Alternatively, you can use the *dayfirst=* function to tell Pandas to interpret this date as August 25, 2019:

```
pd.to_datetime('25/8/2019, dayfirst=True)
```

```
Timestamp('2019-08-25 00:00:00')
```

If you have columns with dates, you can use the *Parse_dates=['date']* function to make the data in that field parsed as the date.

Reading Time Series Data in Pandas package

You can import any .csv program into your Python program. Pandas' `read_csv()` method allows you to read a .csv file or any spreadsheet format used. The function imports data into Pandas DataFrame.

Assume you have the following *sales.csv* file; you can import this file into your Python program and manipulate it.

	A	B	C	D
1		Date	Value	
2	0	7/1/1991	3.526591	
3	1	8/1/1991	3.180891	
4	2	9/1/1991	3.252221	
5	3	10/1/1991	3.611003	
6	4	11/1/1991	3.565869	
7				
8				

Open your IDE and type in the following code:

```
from dateutil.parser import parse

import matplotlib as mpl

import matplotlib.pyplot as plt

import seaborn as sns

import numpy as np

import pandas as pd

plt.rcparams.update({'figure.figsize': (10, 7), 'figure.dpi':120})

dframe=pd.read_csv('sales.csv', parse_dates=['date']

dframe. head()
```

	date	value
0	1991-07-01	3.526591
1	1991-08-01	3.180891
2	1991-09-01	3.252221
3	1991-10-01	3.611003
4	1991-11-01	3.565869

Plotting Time Series Data in Python

Time series visualization plays an important role in data analysis and forecasting. Plots of raw data can provide insights into trends, cycles, performance, and relationships between variables. Visualization of data can be in the form of graphs, line plots, histograms, etc.

Using the daily minimum temperature dataset, this is how to use the dataset for time series visualization. You can download a sample file to practise this code by clicking on this link.

If you're reading the paperback, you can obtain this dataset at:

https://raw.githubusercontent.com/jbrownlee/Datasets/master/daily-min-temperatures.csv

```
from pandas import read_csv
from matplotlib import pyplot
#Display dataset for default 5 rows
temp= read_csv('daily-minimum-temperatures.csv',
            header=0, index_col=0, parse_dates=True, squeeze=True)
print(temp.head())
```

When you run this dataset, it will print the **first 5 rows** of the daily-minimum-temperature dataset.

```
Date
1981-01-01 20.7
1981-01-02 17.9
1981-01-03 18.8
1981-01-04 14.6
1981-01-05 15.8
Name: Temp, dtype: float64
```

We can now plot a line graph to represent the data.

```
from pandas import read_csv

from matplotlib import pyplot

temp = read_csv('daily-minimum-temperatures.csv',

        header=0, index_col=0, parse_dates=True, squeeze=True)

temp.plot()

pyplot.show()
```

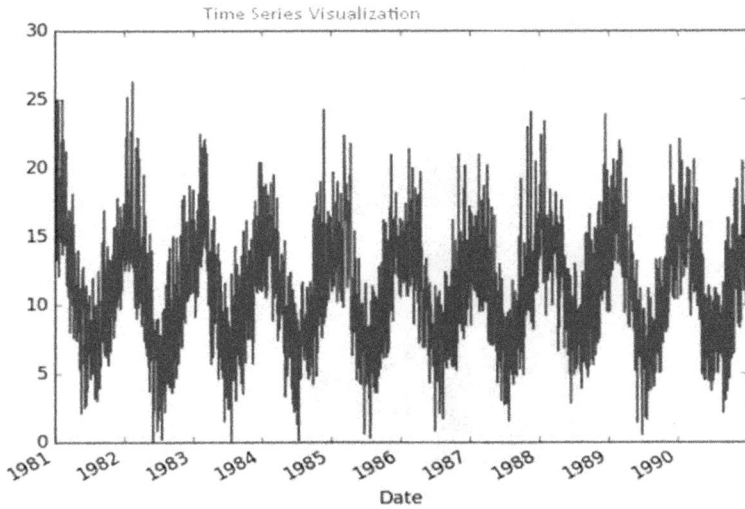

Time Series Visualization

Minimum Daily Temperature Line Plot

Time Series Data Plotted Using a Histogram

```
from pandas import read_csv

from matplotlib import pyplot

temp = read_csv('daily-minimum-temperatures.csv',

        header=0, index_col=0, parse_dates=True, squeeze=True)

temp.hist()

pyplot.show()
```

31

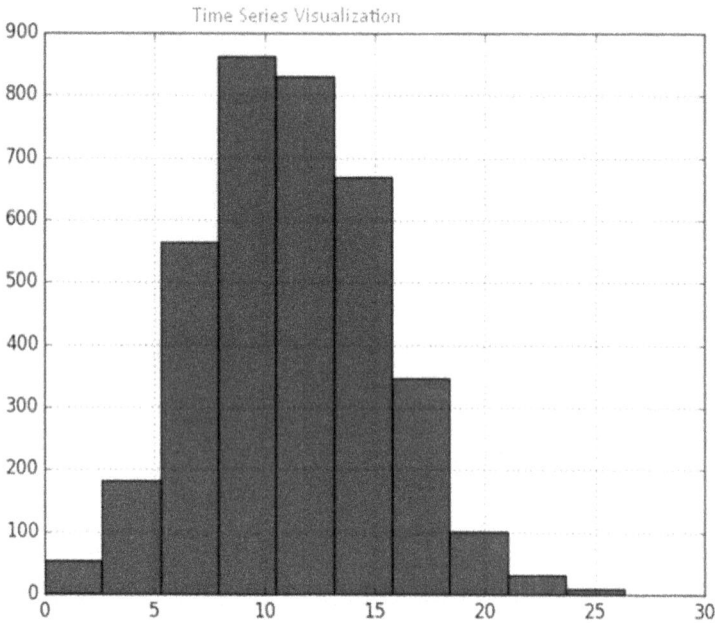

Minimum Daily Temperature Histogram Plot

Chapter Summary

In this chapter, we learned about various trading strategies you can use when investing in the stock market.

- Seven principles to guide you in your daily trading.

- Time series data and how to use it.

- Importing time series data into Python.

In the next chapter, you will learn how to install and set up the Python program into your device.

Setting Up the Workspace

Setting up your workspace does not have to be rocket science and is something you can do entirely on your own. There are requirements that you will need, such as an **Integrated Development Environment (IDE)** and **Python** with you. In this chapter, we will go over the easiest way to set up your workspace for Python.

Using Anaconda is a nice way of starting out. **Anaconda** is a high-performing distribution of both the R and Python programming languages. With it comes hundreds of popular Scala, R, and Python packages you can use for data science. That's not all—there are lots of other benefits accrued with Anaconda too. Installing it will give you access to over 720 other packages for your data science work and any other statistical data. You will also have access to **Jupyter Notebook** and **Spyder IDE**.

Compared to other programming languages, many beginners prefer Python. It has a myriad of libraries with many modules that enable you to analyze your stock data without the need for writing the function code.

Essential Components of Python

Anaconda: Downloading and installing individual libraries and tools needed for your statistical data may be tedious, thus, we need to install Anaconda. Anaconda has all the tools and libraries needed to execute any Python code, with various Python packages to load directly to your IDE framework.

Spyder IDE: Spyder IDE acts as the code editor or software platform where you would write and execute your program codes. The IDE (Integrated Development Environment) not only presents you with the code window to write your code, but it also has a compiler and interpreter used to convert the human-readable code to machine-readable language. It has a debugger program that scans your program for any bugs or errors in the code.

Jupyter Notebook: This is an open-source program that enables you to write and implement program codes in a more interactive format. Jupyter Notebook is used to test a small program code, whereas Spyder IDE is preferable when dealing with multi-file projects.

Conda: Installing Conda will enable you to update your libraries easier. It acts as a management system that automatically installs, runs, and updates your library.

Spyder IDE and Jupyter Notebook will install automatically once you install Anaconda, as they are parts of the Anaconda Distribution.

Installation Process

Step 1

Open the Anaconda website. Click on the version you want to download based on your operating system and system specifications (64-bit and 32-bit).

In this tutorial, we will be downloading Anaconda for **Windows**.

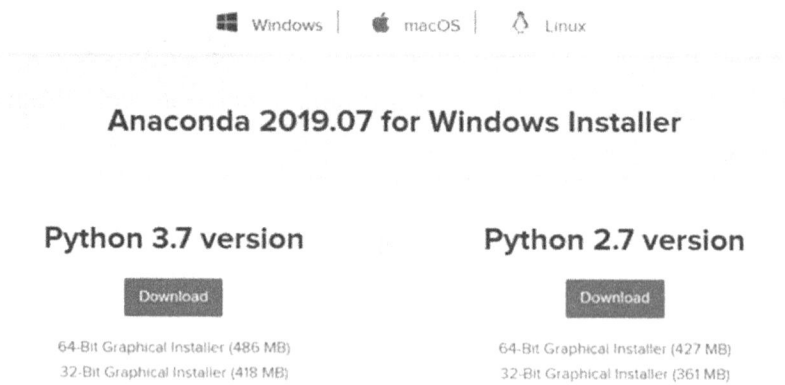

Windows | macOS | Linux

Anaconda 2019.07 for Windows Installer

Python 3.7 version

Download

64-Bit Graphical Installer (486 MB)
32-Bit Graphical Installer (418 MB)

Python 2.7 version

Download

64-Bit Graphical Installer (427 MB)
32-Bit Graphical Installer (361 MB)

Step 2

Once the download is complete, locate the download file and click it to run it.

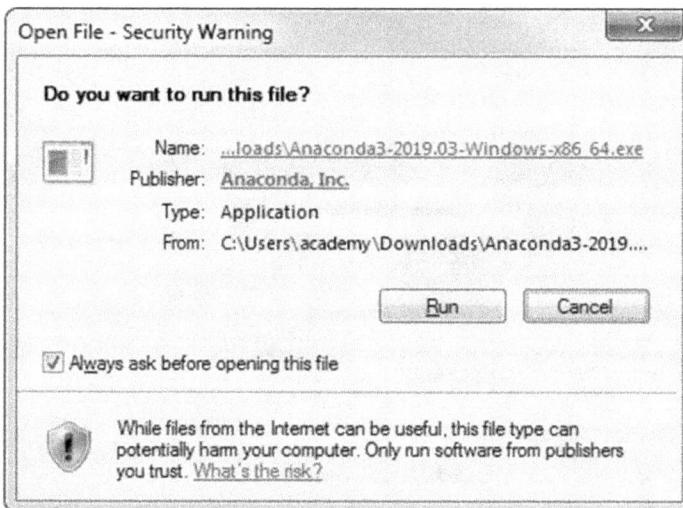

Click **Run** to start the installation.

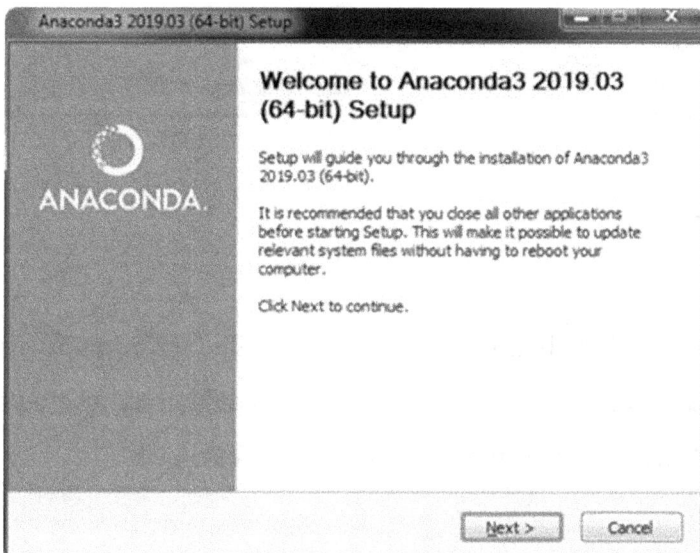

Click **Next** on the opened installation wizard and accept the agreement terms by clicking **I Agree**.

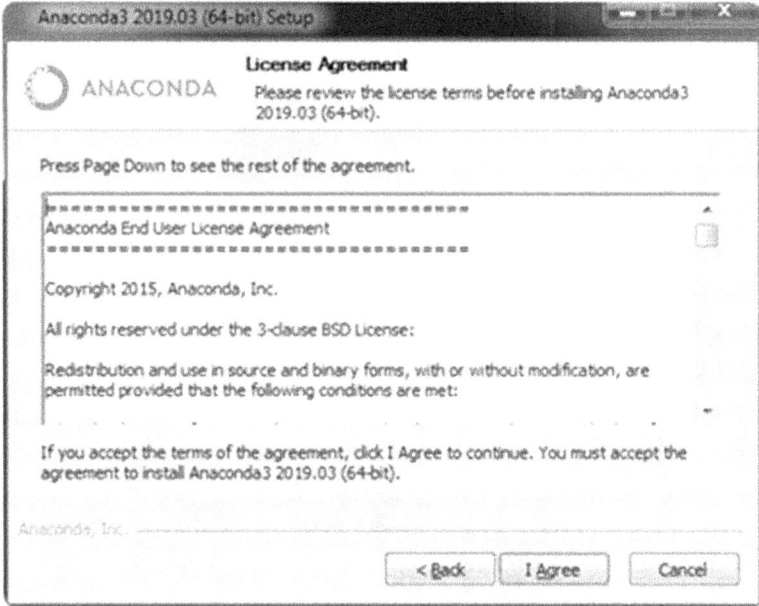

Step 3

Under the Installation type, select **Just Me (recommended)**, then click **Next**. You want to **Save the file**. You can specify where you want to save Anaconda (via **Browse**), then click **Next**.

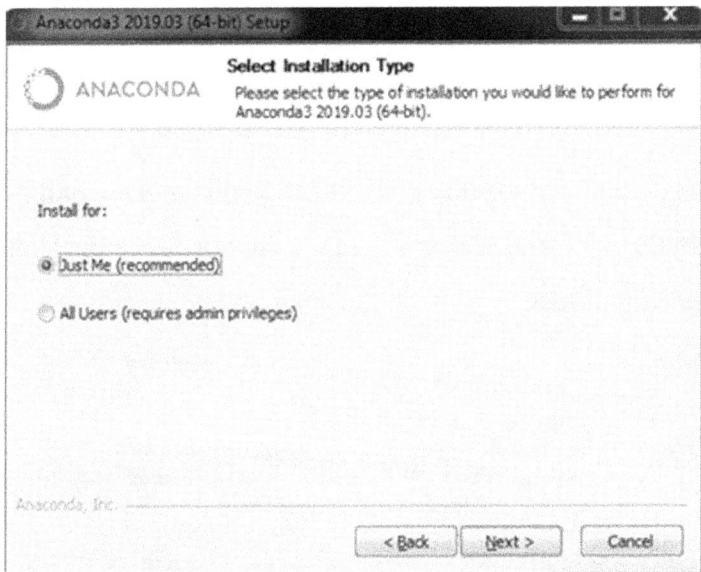

Anaconda3 2019.03 (64-bit) Setup

Select Installation Type

ANACONDA   Please select the type of installation you would like to perform for Anaconda3 2019.03 (64-bit).

Install for:

◉ Just Me (recommended)

○ All Users (requires admin privileges)

Anaconda, Inc.

< Back   Next >   Cancel

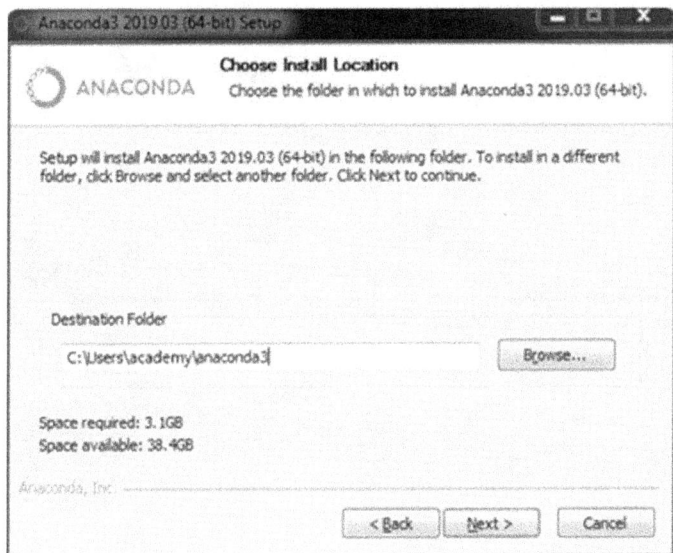

Anaconda3 2019.03 (64-bit) Setup

Choose Install Location

ANACONDA   Choose the folder in which to install Anaconda3 2019.03 (64-bit).

Setup will install Anaconda3 2019.03 (64-bit) in the following folder. To install in a different folder, click Browse and select another folder. Click Next to continue.

Destination Folder

C:\Users\academy\anaconda3   Browse...

Space required: 3.1GB
Space available: 38.4GB

Anaconda, Inc.

< Back   Next >   Cancel

Step 4

Under **Advanced Options**, select the **Register Anaconda as my default Python 3.7** check box, then click **Install**. Once installation is complete, click **Finish**.

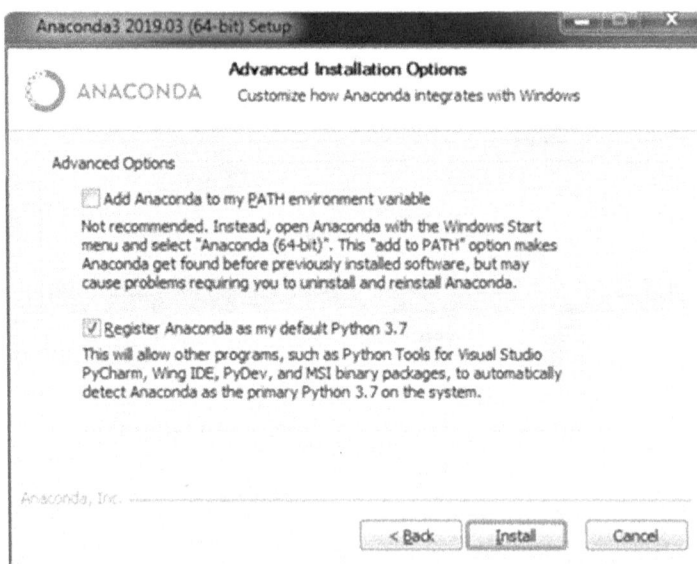

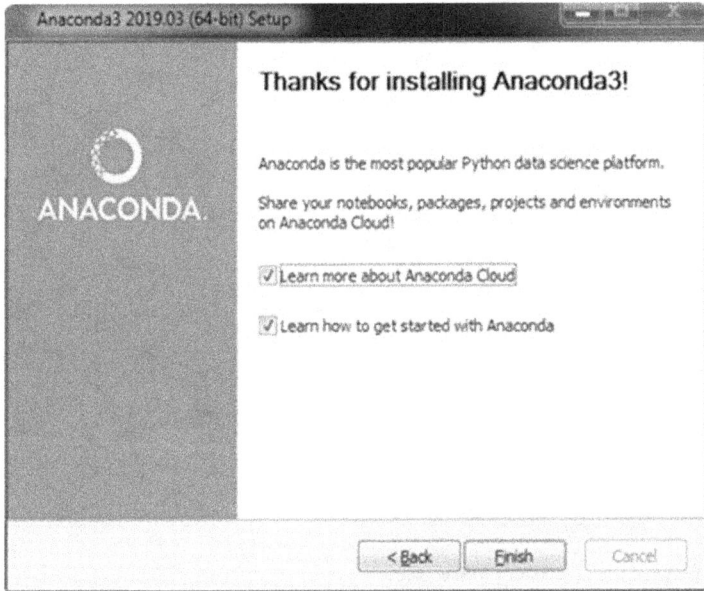

After successfully installing Anaconda, you can open the program navigator and see some of the already installed tools like Jupyter Notebook and Spyder IDE.

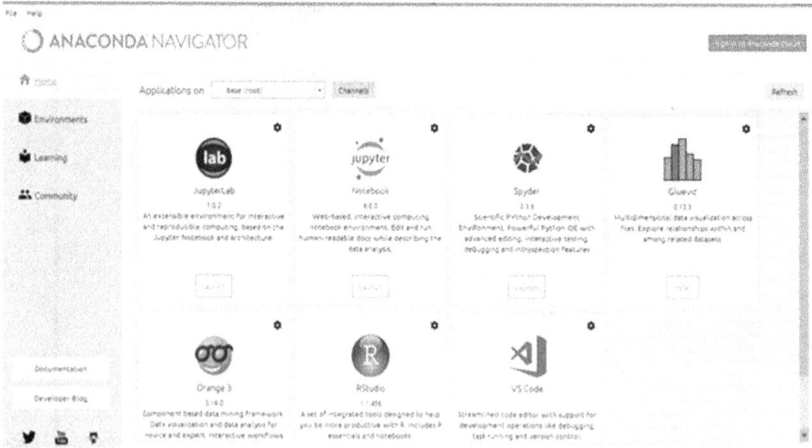

If you're using **MacOS** or **Linux**, you can find installation details on the official Anaconda website.

Chapter Summary

In this chapter, we went over the step-by-step process for installing Anaconda and learned about the various components essential for running the Python program.

Python Basics for Finance

Python for finance allows you to use various data manipulation packages to perform functions such as analyzing statistical data, visualization, and machine learning, among others. In this tutorial, we will focus on libraries required for coding trading strategies and other popular libraries for finance.

A library comprises reusable modules and functions that can perform specific functions. There is no need to write code from scratch for these functions, making Python easy-to-use in data and time series analysis.

Python Packages/Libraries

Pandas: Pandas represent data in the form of a **DataFrame**, with tables or spreadsheet format where you would store data in rows and columns. It allows you to import data directly from an Excel or .csv file into the Python code window. This makes it easy to do data analysis and manipulation of the tabular data.

NumPy: The NumPy library, or **NumericalPy**, is used to perform any numeral calculation on arrays of data. In programming, we call a group of elements an **array**. We can perform different operations using the function NumPy on array elements.

43

Matplotlib: If you want to plot 2D graphs like line charts, bar charts, histograms, and other charts, we call the *Matplotlib* function. The library has various functions that allow you to customize or modify the graph based on your preferences.

Zipline: We use the Zipline library in trading applications. It is an open-source, event-driven system that allows you to receive live trading patterns and perform backtesting of trading strategies.

Technical Analysis Library: Technical Analysis library, or simply **TA-Lib**, allows you to perform technical analysis on financial data. It uses technical indicators like the **Relative Strength Index (RSI)**, **Bollinger Band**s, and **MACD**, among others for analysis.

These Python libraries are ideal for bank analysts and stockbrokers for perfecting their trading strategies.

How to Work with Data in the Python Program

Knowing how to use Python in retrieving data or formatting data is essential for any financial analysis and trading activity.

Python Pandas allows you to analyze time-series data easily and to import data from an Excel file or CSV file format. Investors commonly refer to trading data as time series data because the file would usually index by time (yearly, monthly, weekly, daily, or by the minute).

To carry out any data manipulation and analysis, we need to:

- Import financial data

- Perform numerical analysis

- Build trading strategies based on time series data values

- Plot graphs (time series graphs)

- Perform backtesting on the data

Importing Financial Data in Python

In the following sections, we will import data from different sources using Pandas package.

How to Import CSV Files

The Pandas library has a lot of CSV parsing capabilities that allow you to carry out any numerical analysis. You don't have to build a **CSV parser** from scratch.

CSV file format is a convenient way to export large volumes of data from a spreadsheet or database. We can import this data to use it in another program. When importing CSV files, ensure $pd.DataFrame()$ has the same CSV source file.

Pandas DataFrame makes reading CSV files a quick and straightforward process.

Syntax

```
import pandas as pd


df = pd.read_csv (r' Path to the CSV file stored in your
device/Filename.csv')
print (df)
```

This is a general code for opening any CSV file in Python. You only need to change your CSV file path and run the program.

The `pd.read_csv ()` opens, analyzes, and reads the contents of the CSV file name and stores this data into DataFrame.

Example

The table below shows a list of stock prices for four companies stored in a CSV file (with file name as *NSE_listing.csv*).

	A	B	C	D	E
1	Stock Prices per share				
2	Company	2017 Prices	2018 Price	2019 Prices	
3	Safaricom PLC	$25	$28	$30	
4	Telcom Kenya	$18	$20	$19	
5	Mumias Sugar ltd A	$15	$20	$12	
6	Kenya orchards ltd	$20	$26	$38	
7	Flame tree group holdings	$15	$10	$17	
8	Carbacid Investments ltd	$28	$20	$24	
9	East Africa Breweries ltd	$19	$25	$24	
10	Total	$140	$149	$164	
11					

The following steps outline how to import this file using Python Pandas.

Step 1: Capture the CSV File Path

This is the path where the file is stored. In this case, the file is stored under the following path:

C:/Users/Faith/Documents/NSE_listing.csv

Make sure the file name written in the code matches the file name of your stored file and that it has the **.csv file extension**. This is essential when importing CSV files.

Step 2: Write the Python Code

Open your Python IDE framework to type the code.

```
import pandas as pd

df=pd.read_csv(r'c:\Users\Faith\Documents\NSE_li
sting.csv')

print (df)
```

Step 3: Run Your Code

When you run the code, you will get something like this:

Company	2017 Prices	2018 Prices	2019 Prices
Safaricom PLC	$25.00	$28.00	$30.00
Telcom Kenya	$18.00	$20.00	$19.00
Mumias Sugar ltd A	$15.00	$20.00	$12.00
Kenya orchards ltd	$20.00	$26.00	$38.00
Flame tree group holdings	$15.00	$10.00	$17.00
Carbacid Investments ltd	$28.00	$20.00	$24.00
East Africa Breweries ltd	$19.00	$25.00	$24.00
Total	$140.00	$149.00	$164.00

Customizing the CSV File

You can customize your CSV file and choose only specific rows or columns that interest you.

Let's write a code that will only display the company and 2018 stock prices from NSE_listing.csv file.

```
import pandas as pdr

df=pdr.read_csv(r'c:\Users\Faith\Documents\NSE_l
isting.csv')

df=pdr.DataFrame(data,columns=['company', '2018
prices'])

print (df)
```

Company	2018 Prices
Safaricom PLC	$28.00
Telcom Kenya	$20.00
Mumias Sugar ltd A	$20.00
Kenya orchards ltd	$26.00
Flame tree group holdings	$10.00
Carbacid Investments ltd	$20.00
East Africa Breweries ltd	$25.00
Total	$149.00

Once you import the data into Python, you can start statistical calculations using Pandas.

Data Manipulation Using Time Series Data

Data manipulation is a technique used in organizing data to make it easier to read. You can easily manipulate large volumes of data using the Pandas library. In this example, we will use time series data to analyze data and present it in an orderly manner.

We will use **open system data** (**OPSD**) on *power consumption* in *Germany*. This dataset has a countrywide power consumption for the period between 2007 and 2017. To follow up with the example, download the dataset here.

Let's start by reading the OPSD file:

```
#read opsd file

opsd_daily = pd.read_csv('opsd_germany_daily.csv')

opsd_daily.head(3)#to return the first three rows

opsd_daily.shape #displaying power consumption for three units
```

	Date	Consumption	Wind	Solar	Wind+Solar
0	2006-01-01	1069.184	NaN	NaN	NaN
1	2006-01-02	1380.521	NaN	NaN	NaN
2	2006-01-03	1442.533	NaN	NaN	NaN

When you run this code, it will return the number of rows in the dataset. The *head()* function tells the dataframe to display the first three rows in the dataset.

Customization of Time Series Data

To customize the data, we will import **Matplotlib** for plotting data, and **Seaborn library**, which will provide us with unique ways for styling and adding appropriate size to the plots.

```
import matplotlib.pyplot as plt

import seaborn as sns

# Use seaborn library for defaults styles and set the default
figure size of the plot

sns.set(rc={'figure.figsize':(10, 4)})

opsd_daily['Consumption'].plot(linewidth=0.5);
```

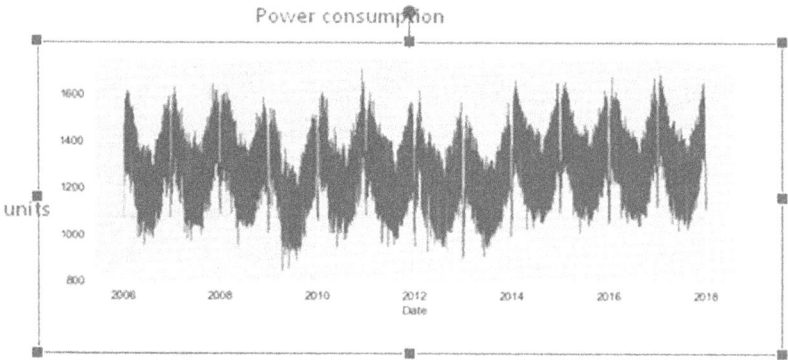

Power consumption

units

| | 2006 | 2008 | 2010 | 2012 | 2014 | 2016 | 2018 |

1600
1400
1200
1000
800

Date

From this plot, you can see that the line plot is too crowded because there are too many data points, making it hard to read. We can solve this by plotting the data in the form of dots and separating the power consumption into *solar* and *wind*.

```
import matplotlib.pyplot as plt

import seaborn as sns


#power consumption for solar and wind

cols_plot = ['Consumption', 'Solar', 'Wind']

#change plot color and set figuresize

axes = opsd_daily[cols_plot].plot(marker='.', alpha=0.5,
linestyle='None', figsize=(10, 9), subplots=True)

#plotting daily power consumption

for ax in axes:

    ax.set_ylabel('Daily Totals (GWh)')
```

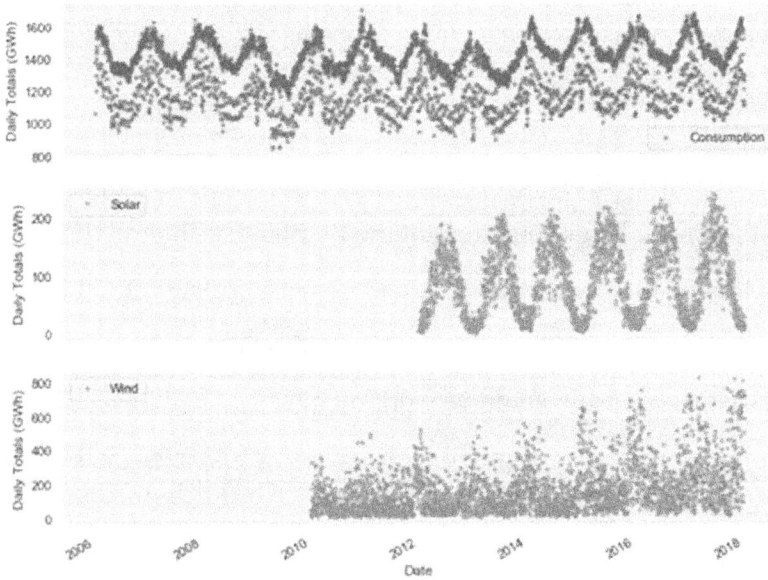

From the plot, we can see that there is high consumption in winter because of increased heating. Wind energy production is also high in winter and low in summer, and so is electricity. Solar production is also high during summer periods.

Importing Google Finance

You can also use Python to download financial data from Google sources or free online databases. Once we download the data, we can use the Python Pandas package for data manipulation and manipulate the data. We then create some data indicators that we can use for the basis of quantitative analysis.

Once you install Anaconda, it will automatically install Pandas and Matplotlib packages. If for some reason the Python distribution does not include them, you can use the `pip` and `conda` packages to install. If you already have the Pandas package installed, you only need to import it into the new project you're working on.

If you're using a non-Anaconda program, you can use `Pandas_datareader (pip install Pandas-datareader)` package and `matplotlib` package for data visualization.

To test whether the `pip install Pandas` command works, open the *'cmd.exe'* command prompt and type: `pip install Pandas`.

If you're using Windows 64-bit, you will get an error message that *'pip' is not recognized as an internal or external command.* Don't worry, as this only means that the `pip` command is not on your path.

You can change the command path to *C:/User/Abi/Python34/Scripts/pip install Pandas* and run the command. *Python34* in the command path means you're using Python 3.4. If you're using version 3.7 and so on, the code will change to *Python37*.

If you installed your Python program via Anaconda, you can install all the additional models using *conda install <module name>*. Add the program path to your file and replace the module name with the actual name of the module you want to install.

In this tutorial, I have installed Anaconda, so to install a module, I will use the *conda* install command.

C:/Users/Abi/Anaconda3/Scripts/conda install Pandas

```
                          C:\Windows\System32\cmd.exe              _ □  ×
operable program or batch file.

C:\Windows\System32>C:/users/faith/Anaconda3/Scripts/conda install pandas
Traceback (most recent call last):
  File "C:\users\faith\Anaconda3\lib\site-packages\conda\exceptions.py", line 10
62, in _call_
    return func(*args, **kwargs)
  File "C:\users\faith\Anaconda3\lib\site-packages\conda\cli\main.py", line 84,
in _main
    exit_code = do_call(args, p)
  File "C:\users\faith\Anaconda3\lib\site-packages\conda\cli\conda_argparse.py",
line 80, in do_call
    module = import_module(relative_mod, __name__.rsplit('.', 1)[0])
  File "C:\users\faith\Anaconda3\lib\importlib\__init__.py", line 127, in import
_module
    return _bootstrap._gcd_import(name[level:], package, level)
  File "<frozen importlib._bootstrap>", line 1006, in _gcd_import
  File "<frozen importlib._bootstrap>", line 983, in _find_and_load
  File "<frozen importlib._bootstrap>", line 967, in _find_and_load_unlocked
  File "<frozen importlib._bootstrap>", line 677, in _load_unlocked
  File "<frozen importlib._bootstrap_external>", line 728, in exec_module
  File "<frozen importlib._bootstrap>", line 219, in _call_with_frames_removed
  File "C:\users\faith\Anaconda3\lib\site-packages\conda\cli\main_install.py", l
ine 8, in <module>
    from .install import install
```

We can now write a code to import data:

```
import Pandas as pd

import datetime

import matplotlib.pyplot as plt

import Pandas_datareader.data as web
```

The `Import Pandas as pd` command imports the Pandas module. *Import datetime* is for when we want to retrieve data based on specific dates and tells Pandas module which dates data it needs to generate.

If you pulled the data from the Internet, use the web command `import Pandas.io.data.`

Once you import the data, you can find data on any free online source such as Google Finance or Yahoo Finance.

In this tutorial, we will use **Google Finance** to obtain market data.

To import Google Finance, you need to install the *googlefinance.client* library. *googlefinance.client* is a Python client library for *google finance api.*

Installing the Library

```
pip install googlefinance.client

or

$ conda install googlefinance.client


#import the libraries
import Pandas as pd
import datetime


import Pandas_datareader.data as web  #to import data from
internet

#Extract price data and time-series data from googlefinance.client

from googlefinance.client import get_price_data, get_prices_data,
get_prices_time_data

# create stock data variables

param = {

    'q': ".DJI", # represent Stock symbol (ex: "AAPL")

    'i': "86400", # Show time Interval size in seconds ("86400" =
1 day intervals)

    'x': "INDEXDJX", # Show type of traded Stock (example: "NASD")

    'p': "1Y" # represent Period in which stocks are traded(Ex:
"1Y" = 1 year)

}

# get price data (return data stored in Pandas dataframe)

df = get_price_data(param)

print(df)
```

Output

	Open	High	Low	Close	Volume
2016-05-17 05:00:00	17531.76	17755.8	17531.76	17710.71	88436105
2016-05-18 05:00:00	17701.46	17701.46	17469.92	17529.98	103253947
2016-05-19 05:00:00	17501.28	17636.22	17418.21	17526.62	79038923
2016-05-20 05:00:00	17514.16	17514.16	17331.07	17435.4	95531058
2016-05-21 05:00:00	17437.32	17571.75	17437.32	17500.94	111992332
...	...	...	...	...	...

Example 2

Here, we will use Google Finance to obtain market data. We will use **ETF "SPY"** as the proxy for **S&P 500**.

```python
# import library

import Pandas as pd

import datetime

import Pandas_datareader.data as web

from googlefinance.client import get_price_data, get_prices_data,
get_prices_time_data


# params = [
    # obtaining market data
    {'q': ".DJI", 'x': "INDEXDJX",},
    # Type of stock traded
    {'q': "NYA", 'x': "INDEXNYSEGIS",},
    # S&P 500
    {'q': ".INX", 'x': "INDEXSP",}]
period = "1Year"
# extract stock volume dataframe [open, high, low, and close,
volume data]
df = get_prices_data(params, period)
print(df)
```

	.DJI_Open	.DJI_High	.DJI_Low	.DJI_Close	.DJI_Volume
2016-07-20	18503.12	18562.53	18495.11	18559.01	85840786
2016-07-21	18582.70	18622.01	18555.65	18595.03	93233337
2016-07-22	18589.96	18590.44	18469.67	18517.23	86803016
2016-07-23	18524.15	18571.30	18491.59	18570.85	87706622
2016-07-26	18554.49	18555.69	18452.62	18493.06	76807470
...	...	...	...	...	...

Use of Excel Spreadsheet in Data Manipulation

Excel is a great tool for data manipulation and analysis. If you do a lot of data cleaning and reformatting, you may find integration of excel Python scripting language is of great use. But there is a lot of data manipulation you can do using the simple excel spreadsheet.

You can use various excel features to manipulate data like filtering an excel report into specific fields of interest or use excel function to perform statistical and mathematical calculations.

A basic excel manipulation range from inserting and deleting columns in an excel spreadsheet or just moving data from one column to another. Whereas in advanced data manipulation, you can create several worksheets, copy pasting data from one worksheet to another or using excel functions to manipulate data from worksheet 1 in worksheet 2.

Excel terminologies

Workbook: This is an excel file that houses all data created in the worksheets. It enables you to manipulate the data entered in the sheets or do some calculations. Once you open an excel app, it automatically opens a workbook you can work on and allow you to store your data.

Worksheet: A worksheet is a sheet within a workbook. You can have more than one worksheet in a workbook. Whenever you open a new worksheet, it creates a tab at the bottom of the screen. The tab also shows the active worksheet you're working on. You can also rename the sheet to make it easy to identify each worksheet.

Rows and columns: They show how data is aligned in the cells. In a row, cells are aligned horizontally while a column is aligned vertically.

Cell: It is a rectangular box that used to enter data. A cell consists of numerical values or text data. An active cell is one that is opened for editing and is referenced by its row and column number. For example, cell A2 points to the first row and second column of your sheet.

Workspace: Just like in worksheet where you can open worksheets, a workspace enables you to work on multiple files simultaneously.

Cell range: This is a group of cells in a worksheet which are selected based on a certain criteria. A colon is put between the selected cell references. For example, A2:C4 is a range of cells that tells excel formula to look for data between the cells A2 and C4.

Manipulating Rows and Columns

When you want to manipulate any data in excel, you have to select a range of cells with data that you want to manipulate. Once you select a row or column, you can cut/copy and paste data in those cells. You can also insert new rows and columns to the left or right of the selected row/column.

You can delete a row or column from the worksheet. Deleting a row or column removes that row or column entirely and collapse the entire sheet making the remaining rows/column take up space for the deleted row /column.

Hide and unhide rows and columns. If you have a large spreadsheet you're working on, you can temporarily hide and unhide rows/columns not needed at the moment. This makes it easy to manage the spreadsheet as you work on it.

Format cells within a row/column by either changing text color, font, background colors or text alignment.

Excel menu offers you multiple tools you can use to manipulate data like applying conditional formatting to your data, create pivot reports or use charts for data visualization and use of excel formulas for mathematical calculations or handling statistical data.

Another way to manipulate excel data is through the use of filters.When filtering data, you have to select the rows/columns you want to filter then from the home menu tool you can filter selected rows/column based on a certain criteria.

For advanced data manipulation, you can integrate excel with Python and perform further manipulation.

How to Integrate Python Data with Excel

Microsoft Excel is a powerful spreadsheet application that allows you to produce and work with lots of mathematical and statistical datasets. When working with large volumes of data, your tasks in Excel may become repetitive, which can consume a lot of your time.

You can rectify this problem by automating your Excel task. You can integrate an Excel spreadsheet with a Python program to modify your files and avoid repetitive work. The **openpyxl module** allows you to read and modify your Excel files.

Openpyxl library also makes it easy to call external functions from Excel like COM objects. In using openpyxl, you don't have to go through a thousand rows to find specific ones based on your criteria. Python eliminates the boring and repetitive tasks.

Installing Openpyxl Module

You can view Python documentation on how to install third-party modules into the Python program. To install the openpyxl module, you would simply type `conda install openpyxl` in your IDE. The command would look like this:

```
C:/Users/Faith/Anaconda3/Scripts/conda install openpyxl
```

Once you install the module, you can test whether it is installed properly by typing the following command in your code editor or IDE:

```
>>>import openpyxl
```

If you have succeeded in installing the module, there will be no error message returned when you type the command on the interactive shell.

Creating a Simple Excel Worksheet

```
from open openpyxl import Workbook
workbook = Workbook()
sheet = workbook.active


#insert data into your sheet 1 under cell A1 and B1
sheet["A1"] = "hello"
sheet["B1"] = "world!"


#display the entered data
workbook.save(filename="hello_world.xlsx")
```

This code will create an Excel sheet with the file name "Hello_world.xlsx".

If you open the file in Excel, this is what you will see:

Reading Excel Documents with Openpyxl

Assume that you have an Excel file called "**fruits.xlsx**" with the following data:

You can open the above file using Python openpyxl module. Type the code below to help open fruits.xlsx by calling *openpyxl.load_workbook()* function.

```
import openpyxl

wb = openpyxl.load_workbook('fruits.xlsx')#opening excel file on a
workbook wb.

type(wb)

<class 'openpyxl.workbook.workbook.Workbook'>
```

The function *openpyxl.load_workbook()* opens the filename and returns a value of the workbook data type. You can also use *workbook.sheetnames* to display the available worksheets.

After opening the spreadsheet, you can easily retrieve specific data from a cell or row. If you need the data in **cell A4**, you can easily retrieve it like this:

```
# retrieve data from cells

sheet.cell(row=4, column=2)

<Cell 'Sheet 1'.A4>


sheet.cell(row=4, column=2).value
```

68

You can also loop the function to print a series of values in a specific range:

```
# retreive data from cell A2
sheet.cell(row2, column=1)
<Cell Sheet1.A2>
sheet.cell(row=2, column=1).value


#printing data in cells in the range of 1,8,2
 for i in range(1, 8, 2):
    print(i, sheet.cell(row=i, column=1).value)
```

Output

```
         output

         1 Apples
         3 Pears
         5 Apples
         7 Strawberries
```

Calling the `cell()` method and passing it to `row=2`, `column=1` will display the object in **cell A2**. You would use the `for` loop to print a series of cells based on specific criteria.

Always make sure you supply the exact path to the filename in your code; otherwise, it will generate an error code if the file path is different from the one you wrote in the code.

Dealing with Different Worksheets

If your workbook has data from different worksheets, you can receive data from each worksheet by using the `get_sheet_names()` function.

Example

```
import openpyxl
wb = openpyxl.load_workbook('fruits.xlsx')
wb.get_sheet_names()
['Sheet1', 'Sheet2', 'Sheet3']
#specify the sheet name to get data
sheet = wb.get_sheet_by_name('Sheet3')
sheet <Worksheet "Sheet3">
type(sheet) <class 'openpyxl.worksheet.worksheet.Worksheet'>
sheet.title
# set up active worksheet
anotherSheet = wb.active
anotherSheet
<Worksheet "Sheet1">
```

You can call each worksheet by passing the worksheet name string to `get_sheet_names()`.

You can set any of the worksheet to be at the top anytime you open your workbook by using `.active` feature.

Importing Data from Excel File into Pandas

You can read data from an Excel file using Pandas module. To do this, you need to first import data from your Excel file into Pandas module:

```
Import Pandas as pd
```

After importing, you can then use the `read_Excel()` function to read the data from the Excel file. You can do this by calling the Excel file name using the following command.

```
Excel_file='fruits.xlsx'
Fruits=pd.read_Excel(Excel_file)
```

The call to function `read_Excel()` reads the Excel data into the Pandas DataFrame object since Pandas stores data in form of

DataFrames. After reading the file, Pandas then stores the DataFrame into the variable `fruits`.

Chapter Summary

In this chapter, we learned how to use Pandas to analyze time series data. We can now also import, export, and manipulate data using Pandas.

You can use **Pandas-reader** to read data files in Google, Yahoo Finance Report, and World Bank.

In the next chapter, we go over how to use time series to manipulate data.

Working With Time Series Data

From the previous chapter, we learned how to import data into our workspace. In this chapter, we will learn how to manipulate data using the Python packages Pandas, NumPy, SciPy, and Matplotlib, among others.

By the end, you will also be able to perform some financial analysis from the data imported into your workspace.

Using Pandas-datareader to Import Data

Over the years, Python has been a great language for data analysis and visualization. It's fantastic ecosystem of packages has been a great help in performing statistical and mathematical functions among other functions. Pandas is one of the most commonly used packages for importing and analyzing data in Python.

The Pandas-datareader function allows you to read data from a variety of sources such as Excel data, CSV files, and web data from sources like Google, Yahoo, and World Bank. The Pandas package will allow you to analyze the CSV files and web data imported to your workspace.

Installing Pandas

To start, install Pandas package into your machine using the `pip` command if using Python, or `conda` if using Anaconda.

```
pip install Pandas
```

or

```
conda install Pandas
```

To read Python data, install the `Pandas-datareader` function:

```
import Pandas_datareader as pdr
```

Example

Let's use `Pandas-datareader` to pull data from a Yahoo page:

```
import Pandas_datareader as pd

import datetime

aapl = pd.get_yahoo_data('AAPL',

                         start_date=datetime.datetime(2011, 10,
1),

                         end_date=datetime.datetime(2019, 10,
1))
```

You can also use **Quandl library** to import data from a web source, such as Google Finance data:

```
import quandl

import datetime

aapl = quandl.get("WIKI/AAPL", start_date="2011-10-01",
end_date="2019-10-01")
```

As we have seen, you can use the *Pandas_datareader* command to extract data from any source into your Python program

The program stores the extracted data in a DataFrame *aapl*,which is a data structure that holds both the rows and columns of your data.

Creating Pandas DataFrame

A DataFrame is a tool used in the representation of data in the form of a table. **Tabular data** is data shown in rows and columns. When importing data into Pandas, you need to load the CSV files into Pandas DataFrame.

To create a DataFrame, you need to pass multiple series of data using the `pd.series` method into DataFrame class. This is like a two-dimensional array.

Example

Here, we will use two series objects: **L1** and **L2**.

```
import pandas as pd

# series variables

L1= pd.Series([1,2])

L2= pd.Series(["Mary", "John"])



#frame the series objects

df= pd.DataFrame([L1,L2])
```

df

	0	1
0	1	2
1	Mary	John

 # create dataset with use of index and column values

df = pd.DataFrame([[1,2],["Mary", "John"]],

   index=["r3", "r4"],

   columns=["c3", "c4"])

df

	C3	C4
r3	1	2
r4	Mary	John

#create dataset with dict-like container

df = pd.DataFrame({

   "c3": [1, "Mary"],

77

```
    "c4": [2, "John"] })
```

df

	C3	C4
0	1	2
1	Mary	John

After creating a DataFrame for your project, you can run the `head()` and `tail()` functions to enable you call the first row and last row of the data stored in the DataFrame.

Example: Importing data from a CSV file to your computer

Assuming you have a file named project_data.csv in your computer, you can easily retrieve it using pandas dataframe. Make sure to use the specific path to the file location.

From the dataframe we can create a code to only retrieve the first 10 rows of data. The head () function returns the first five rows by default. If you need more rows you have to specify the number.

```
import pandas as pd



# read the dataframe and assign into variable df

dframe = pd.read_csv("Project_data.csv")



dframe.head(10)
```

Project Name	Start Date	End Date	Duration	Team Members	Project Budget	Actual Budget
Project A	5/5/2016	7/1/2016	57	10	$1,000,000.00	$880,000.00
Project B	5/10/2016	8/10/2016	92	2	$900,000.00	$920,000.00
Project C	6/10/2016	3/1/2017	264	4	$860,000.00	$880,000.00
Project D	6/22/2016	8/4/2016	43	5	$1,000,000.00	$998,050.00
Project E	7/14/2016	11/1/2016	110	7	$294,000.00	$280,000.00
Project F	7/14/2016	1/20/2017	190	5	$123,400.00	$125,000.00
Project G	8/1/2016	10/1/2016	61	12	$250,500.00	$236,000.00
Project H	8/14/2016	8/30/2016	16	2	$127,200.00	$126,000.00
Project I	9/1/2016	12/10/2016	100	7	$80,000.00	$79,900.00
Project J	10/1/2016	11/15/2016	45	5	$77,000.00	$77,000.00

To print the entire rows and columns in the dataframe we use
`dframe.shape` command

```
import pandas as pd

dframe=pd.read_csv("project_data.csv")

dframe.shape
```

Project Name	Start Date	End Date	Duration	Team Members	Project Budget	Actual Budget
Project A	5/5/2016	7/1/2016	57	10	$1,000,000.00	$880,000.00
Project B	5/10/2016	8/10/2016	92	2	$900,000.00	$920,000.00
Project C	6/10/2016	3/1/2017	264	4	$860,000.00	$880,000.00
Project D	6/22/2016	8/4/2016	43	5	$1,000,000.00	$998,050.00
Project E	7/14/2016	11/1/2016	110	7	$294,000.00	$280,000.00
Project F	7/14/2016	1/20/2017	190	5	$123,400.00	$125,000.00
Project G	8/1/2016	10/1/2016	61	12	$250,500.00	$236,000.00
Project H	8/14/2016	8/30/2016	16	2	$127,200.00	$126,000.00
Project I	9/1/2016	12/10/2016	100	7	$80,000.00	$79,900.00
Project J	10/1/2016	11/15/2016	45	5	$77,000.00	$77,000.00
Project K	10/1/2016	12/1/2016	61	10	$65,000.00	$55,000.00
Project L	11/1/2016	12/1/2016	30	4	$550,000.00	$651,000.00
Project M	11/10/2016	12/10/2016	30	3	$45,000.00	$42,000.00
Project N	12/1/2016	2/10/2017	71	1	$32,500.00	$25,000.00
					$5,404,600.00	$5,374,950.00

Indexing DataFrames in Pandas

Indexing means to extract specific rows and columns of data from the DataFrame. This allows it to customize your file by only reading the specific data needed. In indexing, you can select a specific row and column, or select all the rows and a few columns.

Sometimes we would refer to indexing as a **subset selection**, as you would only select a specific number of rows and columns in the process.

Example

Let's use our *project_data.csv* DataFrame to practice on how to do indexing. Create the file and follow this example to perform indexing.

	Project Name	Start Date	End Date	Duration	# of Team Members	Project Budget	Actual Budget
1							
2	Project A	05/05/16	07/01/16	57	10	$1,000,000	$880,000
3	Project B	05/10/16	08/10/16	92	2	$900,000	$920,000
4	Project C	06/10/16	03/01/17	264	4	$860,000	$880,000
5	Project D	06/22/16	08/04/16	43	5	$1,000,000	$998,050
6	Project E	07/14/16	11/01/16	110	7	$294,000	$280,000
7	Project F	07/14/16	01/20/17	190	5	$123,400	$125,000
8	Project G	08/01/16	10/01/16	61	12	$250,500	$236,000
9	Project H	08/14/16	08/30/16	16	2	$127,200	$126,000
10	Project I	09/01/16	12/10/16	100	7	$80,000	$79,900
11	Project J	10/01/16	11/15/16	45	5	$77,000	$77,000
12	Project K	10/01/16	12/01/16	61	10	$65,000	$55,000
13	Project L	11/01/16	12/01/16	30	4	$550,000	$651,000
14	Project M	11/10/16	12/10/16	30	3	$45,000	$42,000
15	Project N	12/01/16	02/10/17	71	1	$32,500	$25,000
16						$5,404,600	$5,374,950

Assume that you only want to see data from **Project A, Project B, Project C** and the corresponding three columns namely; **project name, start date** and **end date**. You can write a code that will only retrieve the specific data you need from the dataframe.

Project Name	Start Date	End Date
Project A	5/5/2016	7/1/2016
Project B	5/10/2016	8/10/2016
Project C	6/10/2016	3/1/2017

There are different methods you can use to pull data from a DataFrame. Python Pandas library offers three ways of indexing data, with the most common being the `.loc()` and `.iloc()` methods. These methods allow you to retrieve as many rows and columns as you need by their position.

`DataFrame.[]`: This method acts as the **indexing operator**.

`DataFrame.loc[]`: Use the `.loc[]` function when dealing with **labels**.

82

`DataFrame.iloc[]`: The `.iloc[]` method is great for when you're looking for the position of certain DataFrames or when dealing with **integer-based data**.

How to use DataFrame indexing operator *[]*

We designate an operator as the **indexing operator** by following it with square brackets (`[]`). Both `.iloc` and `.loc` use the indexing operator to receive data from different rows and columns.

Example: Selecting a single column from our project_data.csv file

```
import pandas as pd

dframe = pd.read_csv("project_data.csv",
index_col ="Project Name")

# indexing operator to retrieve columns

firstindex = dframe["Duration"]

print(firstindex)
```

Output

Project Name	Duration
Project A	57
Project B	92
Project C	264
Project D	43
Project E	110
Project F	190
Project G	61
Project H	16
Project I	100
Project J	45
Project K	61
Project L	30
Project M	30
Project N	71

project Name: length:15, dtype:float

If you need to select **multiple columns**, you can modify the operator with the specific columns you need to retrieve:

```python
import pandas as pd

dframe = pd.read_csv("project_data.csv",
index_col ="Project Name")

columns = dframe[["Project Name", "Start Date",
"End Date", "Project Budget"]]

print (columns)
```

Project Name	Start Date	End Date	Project Budget
Project A	5/5/2016	7/1/2016	$1,000,000.00
Project B	5/10/2016	8/10/2016	$900,000.00
Project C	6/10/2016	3/1/2017	$860,000.00
Project D	6/22/2016	8/4/2016	$1,000,000.00
Project E	7/14/2016	11/1/2016	$294,000.00
Project F	7/14/2016	1/20/2017	$123,400.00
Project G	8/1/2016	10/1/2016	$250,500.00
Project H	8/14/2016	8/30/2016	$127,200.00
Project I	9/1/2016	12/10/2016	$80,000.00
Project J	10/1/2016	11/15/2016	$77,000.00
Project K	10/1/2016	12/1/2016	$65,000.00
Project L	11/1/2016	12/1/2016	$550,000.00
Project M	11/10/2016	12/10/2016	$45,000.00
Project N	12/1/2016	2/10/2017	$32,500.00

Indexing using *DataFrame.loc[]*

We use the .*loc[]* function to obtain a row or column label. This function operates differently from the indexing operator, as it selects various subsets of rows and columns from the dataset. If you want to select a **single row**, put a single row label inside the square brackets:

```
import pandas as pd

dframe = pd.read_csv("project_data.csv",
index_col ="Project Name")

# retrieve row by loc method

Row2 = dframe.loc["Project B"]

Row3 = dframe.loc["Project C"]

print(row2, "\n\n\n", row3)
```

Project Name	Project B	
Start Date		5/10/2016
End Date		8/10/2016
Duration	92	
# of Team Members		2
Project Budget		$900,000.00
Actual Budget		$920,000.00

Project Name: Project B, dtype: object

Project Name	Project C	
Start Date		6/10/2016
End Date		3/1/2017
Duration	264	
# of Team Members		4
Project Budget		$860,000.00
Actual Budget		$880,000.00

Project Name: Project C, dtype: object

If you need to **import multiple rows**, put the row labels in a list and call the `.loc()` function:

```
import pandas as pd

dframe = pd.read_csv("project_data.csv",
index_col ="Project Name")

#multiple rows
```

88

```
rows = dframe.loc[["Project A", "Project B"]]

print (rows)
```

Project Name	Start Date	End Date	Duration	Team Members	Project Budget	Actual Budget
Project A	5/5/2016	7/1/2016	57	10	$1,000,000.00	$880,000.00
Project B	5/10/2016	8/10/2016	92	2	$900,000.00	$920,000.00

If you want to select **more rows and columns**, modify the `.loc[]` function to fetch data from both rows and columns:

```
import pandas as pd

# Retrieve dataframe csv file

dframe = pd.read_csv("project_data.csv",
index_col ="Project Name")

# retrieving two rows and three columns by loc
method

rowcol = dframe.loc[["Project A", "Project B"],

            ["Start date", "End date",
"Duration"]]

  print(rowcol)
```

89

Project Name	Start Date	End Date	Duration
Project A	5/5/2016	7/1/2016	57
Project B	5/10/2016	8/10/2016	92

Indexing DataFrame using .iloc[]

.iloc[] allows you to retrieve both rows and columns by position. If you need to select data from a certain row or column, specify the row and column position. This ensures that you extract data from only that selected row or column. The .iloc[] function uses an integer number to specify the location of the row or column you select.

```
import pandas as pd


dframe = pd.read_csv("project_data.csv",
index_col ="Project Name")

# .iloc method to retrieve 3 rows

rows = dframe.iloc[3]

print(rows)
```

Extracting data from multiple rows and columns

```python
import pandas as pd

# Retrieve csv dataframe

dframe = pd.read_csv("project_data.csv",
index_col ="Project Name")

# .iloc method to retrieve multiple rows

rows = dframe.iloc [[1, 5],[2, 5]]



print (rows)
```

Project Name	# of Team Members
Project A	10
Project B	2

Using *head()* and *tail()* to Peek at Data

We use the *head ()* and *tail ()* functions to extract data from the **first rows** and the **last rows** of a DataFrame. By default, the *head ()* function returns the **first five rows** of a DataFrame.

Syntax

```
Dataframe.head(n=5)
```

Example

From our **project_data.csv** file, we will return the **top five rows** of the DataFrame and store in a new variable:

```
import pandas as pd

dframe = pd.read_csv("project_data.csv")

top_rows = dframe.head()

print (top_rows)
```

Since the default parameter for *head ()* is 5, you don't have to pass any parameters to the function.

Project Name	Start Date	End Date	Duration f	Team Members	Project Budget	Actual Budget
Project A	5/5/2016	7/1/2016	57	10	$1,000,000.00	$880,000.00
Project B	5/10/2016	8/10/2016	92	2	$900,000.00	$920,000.00
Project C	6/10/2016	3/1/2017	264	4	$860,000.00	$880,000.00
Project D	6/22/2016	8/4/2016	43	5	$1,000,000.00	$998,050.00
Project E	7/14/2016	11/1/2016	110	7	$294,000.00	$280,000.00

Calling **head ()** *with n^{th} number of rows.*

import pandas as pd

df = pd.read_csv("project_data.csv")

n = 9

 # enter data series variable

dataseries = df["Project Name"]

 # return the top 9 rows

top = dataseries.head(n = n)

Print (top)

Project Name

Project A

Project B

Project C

Project D

Project E

Project F

Project G

Project H

Project I

The `tail()` function works similar to the `head()` function, as it returns the **last nth number of rows** in a dataframe.

Syntax

`Dataframe.tail(n)`

Use the same example and replace `head()` function with the `tail()` function to display the last 9 rows in the dataframe.

Where *n* is the number of rows you want returned.

DataFrame *describe* () function

The Pandas `describe()` function is a great data analysis tool that enables you find summarized data. The function can perform basic statistical calculations like calculating **mean, STD**, and **percentile**, among others.

A **percentile** is the nth value in a group of population that is divided into two: the lower value and the upper value. The lower value contain values of n percent of where the data falls whereas the upper part contains the rest of the data. It indicates a value below which a given percentage of observation in a dataset falls. For example, a percentile of 30 is the value in which 30% of the observations fall below that value.

Percentiles are represented by values between 0-100 with 50th percentile being the median.

Syntax

`DataFrame.describe(percentiles=None, include=None, exclude=None)`

Where,

percentiles=: shows list-like datatype of numbers between 0-1 to return the percentile.

include=: displays the list of datatypes to include when describing the DataFrame. Default datatype is **none**.

exclude=: displays the list of datatypes to exclude when describing the DataFrame. Default datatype is **none**.

Return type: the statistical summary of the dataframe.

Example

Employee_details.csv is a file with a list of 364 employees with information about their relevant details. It is not included in this book since it would take up too much space; and it does include personal information that we do not want to disclose.

96

We will create a statistical summary of a DataFrame with both objects and a numeric data type. Using the **Employee_details.csv** file, we will calculate the respective percentile for the object series **[.20, .40, .60, .80].**

import pandas as pd

```python
import pandas as pd
# call function to regex module
import re
data = pd.read_csv ("Employee_details.csv")

# remove null values and set inplace value to true to catch
errors
data.dropna (inplace = True)
perc = [.20, .40, .60, .80]
 # dtypes to retrieve
include = ['int', 'float', 'object']

desc = data.describe (percentiles = perc, include = include)
desc
```

	Name	Team	Number	Position	Age	Height	Weight	College	Salary
count	364	364	364.000000	364	364	364	364.000000	364	3.640000e+02
unique	364	30	NaN	5	22	17	NaN	115	NaN
top	Cleanthony Early	New Orleans Pelicans	NaN	SG	24.0	6-9	NaN	Kentucky	NaN
freq	1	16	NaN	87	41	49	NaN	22	NaN
mean	NaN	NaN	16.829670	NaN	NaN	NaN	219.785714	NaN	4.620311e+06
std	NaN	NaN	14.994162	NaN	NaN	NaN	24.793099	NaN	5.119716e+06
min	NaN	NaN	0.000000	NaN	NaN	NaN	161.000000	NaN	5.572200e+04
20%	NaN	NaN	4.000000	NaN	NaN	NaN	195.000000	NaN	9.472760e+05
40%	NaN	NaN	9.000000	NaN	NaN	NaN	212.000000	NaN	1.638754e+06
50%	NaN	NaN	12.000000	NaN	NaN	NaN	220.000000	NaN	2.515440e+06
60%	NaN	NaN	17.000000	NaN	NaN	NaN	228.000000	NaN	3.429934e+06
80%	NaN	NaN	30.000000	NaN	NaN	NaN	242.400000	NaN	7.838202e+06
max	NaN	NaN	99.000000	NaN	NaN	NaN	279.000000	NaN	2.287500e+07

From the output, you can see that for all the percentile and columns with strings, a **NaN** is returned.

Example 2: Using `describe()` in a series of strings

```
import pandas as pd
# importing regex module
import re
data = pd.read_csv("Employee_details.csv")
data.dropna(inplace = True)
#use describe() to retrieve employee name
desc = data["Name"].describe()
desc
```

When you run the program, it will return unique values and count all the values and the frequency of occurrence, as shown below.

```
Using describe() to count values

count                      364
unique                     364
top          Cleanthony Early
freq                         1
Name: Name, dtype: object
```

DataFrame *Resample()* function

Resample() function is essential for data manipulation. When you have a dataset recorded in a set time interval, you can change the time interval using **the resampling technique**. You may set the time interval to daily, weekly, monthly, or semiannually. You can also resample hourly data into minute-by-minute data.

The function is ideal for frequency conversion and for sampling time series data. In time series data, you would index the data points in a particular time order; thus, *resample()* is a convenient method for resampling time series data.

All objects in the *resample()* method should have a **datetime index** (either a DatetimeIndex, PeriodIndex, or a TimedeltaIndex) or they should pass values in the form of datetime.

Syntax

*DataFrame.**resample(arguments).<aggregate function>***

Resample arguments:

```
DataFrame.resample(rule, how=None, axis=0, fill_method=None,
closed=None, label=None, convention='start', kind=None,
loffset=None, limit=None, base=0, on=None, level=None)
```

Where,

rule: = the offset string or object that represents the **target conversion**. The parameter you use determines the interval by which the program will resample data:
*data.resample('**3min**').sum()*

axis: contains data of *int* type, which is optional. Default value= 0

closed: { *'right'*, *'left'* }

label: { *'right'*, *'left'* }

convention: for PeriodIndex only; it controls whether to use the start or end of the rule.

loffset: a parameter used to adjust the resampled time labels.

base: a parameter for frequencies that evenly subdivide one day; the "origin" of the aggregated intervals. For example, for a "5 min" frequency, the base can range from 0 to 4. Default value= 0.

on: parameter set for column DataFrame instead of index for resampling. Column must be **datetime-like**.

level: For a MultiIndex level (name or number) to use for resampling. Level must be **datetime-like**.

Types of Resampling

Resampling is categorized into two: **downsampling** and **upsampling**.

Downsampling: where the function resamples data from a wider time frame, such as months or years. When downsampling, you can use several groups by aggregating functions like $min()$, $max()$, $sum()$, $means()$, etc.

When you downsample, you reduce the number of rows in the dataframe.

Upsampling: allows you to resample your data for a short period.

Resampling enables you to create a unique distribution of data. For example, if you use time series data with six-minute timestamps, you can *downsample* the time series into three minutes.

Example

We will use the **shares_value.csv** file and `resample()` the data on a **monthly basis**. You can download a sample CSV file from this <u>link.</u>

```
import pandas as pd

# use parse_date function to convert timestamp
column into datetime format.

 parse_dates =["Timestamp"]

# Resampling works well with time-series data
therefore, convert timestamp column to an index
form

  index_col ="Timestamp"

data =pd.read_csv("shares_value.csv",
parse_dates =["Timestamp"], index_col
="Timestamp")

 # Print 12 rows of the shares_value dataframe

data[:12]
```

Timestamp	closing value	volume	open	high	low
12/20/2018	192.23	46541444	191.72	197.18	191.4501
12/13/2018	192.23	46725710	191.63	197.18	191.4501
12/12/2018	194.17	50991030	199	199.85	193.79
12/9/2018	204.47	34317760	205.55	206.01	202.25
11/8/2018	208.49	25289270	209.98	210.12	206.75
11/7/2018	209.95	33291640	205.97	210.06	204.13
11/6/2018	203.77	31774720	201.92	204.72	201.69
11/5/2018	201.59	66072170	204.3	204.39	198.17
11/2/2018	207.48	91046560	209.55	213.65	205.43
11/1/2018	222.22	52954070	219.05	222.36	216.81
10/31/2018	218.86	38016810	216.88	220.45	216.62
10/30/2018	213.3	36487930	211.15	215.18	209.27

With the above data, you can calculate the **mean closing price** for each month.

```
import pandas as pd
```

```
parse_dates =["timestamp"]
```

```python
 index_col ="timestamp"

data =pd.read_csv("shares_value.csv",
parse_dates =["timestamp"], index_col
="timestamp")

#create variable M to represent months and
calculate mean


monthly_resampled_data=data.close.resample('M').
mean()


# Print closing mean for 12 months

data[monthly_resampled_data]
```

```
Resampled mean() for 12 months
date
2017-11-30      172.090769
2017-12-31      171.891500
2018-01-31      174.005238
2018-02-28      167.638947
2018-03-31      174.496190
2018-04-30      169.834286
2018-05-31      185.536818
2018-06-30      188.621429
2018-07-31      190.311429
2018-08-31      213.346087
2018-09-30      222.073684
2018-10-31      220.845652
2018-11-30      204.930000
Freq: M, Name: close, dtype: float64
```

Graph for frequency conversion

import matplotlib.pyplot as plt

plotly.data[monthly_resampled_data]

plt.show()

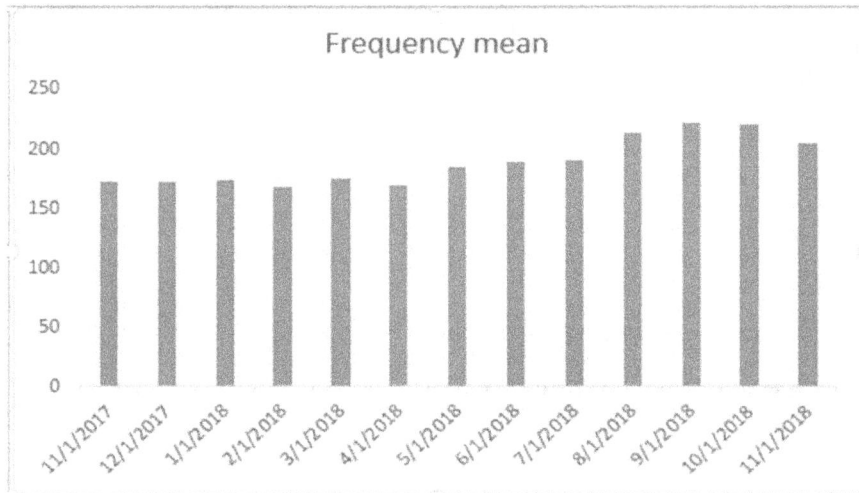

Frequency mean

When resampling data on a **weekly basis**, you can apply the mean opening price to the dataframe.

The code will look like this:

```
Weekly_resampled_data=df.open.resample('n').mean()
```

Chapter Summary

In this chapter, you learned how to work with time series data, with examples. You also learned how to use the *Pandas_datareader()* function to import data into the workspace and carry out statistical functions for analyzing the data. Some of these statistical functions included:

- Using *head()* and *tail()* functions to peek data

- Using *describe()* to generate summary data

- Using *resample()* function for frequency conversion and sampling of time series data

- How to use *.loc()* and *.iloc()* to select data from different columns and rows.

In the next chapter, we will look at how to visualize data using time series, and how to plot time series charts and scatter matrix.

How To Visualize Time Series Data

What is Data Visualization?

Data visualization is a presentation of data in the form of charts or graphs. The plotted graphs make it easy to understand, allowing you to detect trends, patterns, and outliers easily in any group of data.

Data visualization is essential for data analysis and observation of time series data. Over recent years, more companies have been investing in big data and machine learning to analyze large volumes of collected data. Data analysts require tools that will enable them to comprehend and present complex organization data for stakeholders and business owners.

One way to make data more presentable is to convert the complex data into a visual format as compared to having multiple lines of text and numbers.

Data visualization not only saves you the time of going through multiple lines to understand data, but it also makes it easy for you to identify trends in the optimization process.

Python provides you with the tools you need to present visual data. It offers multiple graphical libraries that provide wide features for plotting graphs and charts. You can easily create highly interactive graphics or customize charts based on your needs.

Some of these Python libraries for data visualization include:

Matplotlib: This is a low-level library that gives the freedom to customize your charts based on your needs. To install Matplotlib, you can use both *pip* or *conda*.

```
pip install matplotlib
```

or

```
conda install matplotlib
```

You can use Matplotlib when you want to create basic charts like bar charts, line charts, histograms, and pie charts, among other basic charts.

To use Matplotlib, import the library into your workspace.

Syntax

```
Import Matplotlib.pyplot as plt
```

Pandas Visualization: This is a great, easy-to-use, open-source tool with a high-performance library that can provide lots of data structures. These structures include Dataframes and data visualization tools to analyze and present data. It is built on the Matplotlib library and makes it easy to create plots from stored Pandas DataFrame or series.

Because of its high level of API compared to Matplotlib, the Pandas visualization tool requires less coding.

You can install Pandas through:

```
pip install Pandas
```

or

```
conda install Pandas
```

Seaborn: This is a great visualization tool for high-level interfaces and has plenty of default styles. Using the seaborn library, you can create a graph that can read data from multiple lines in Matplotlib. It has an interactive interface that gives an opportunity to work with Pandas DataFrames.

To use this library, import it to your IDE interface.

```
import seaborn as sns
```

Plotly: Plotly is an advanced data visualization tool that includes the Python API libraries. The tool integrates with Python to make interactive web-based apps. Install the library to your device by running the *pip* or *conda* install.

```
pip install plotly
```

or

```
conda install plotly
```

Once you install plotly, you have to authenticate the library and replace the username and API key.

```
import plotly.plotly as py


# Authenticate account with your username and password

plotly.tools.set_credentials_file(username='enter username',

                                api_key='enter password')
```

If you plan to use plotly online, you need to create an account with a username. A free plotly account allows you to create 25 public charts and one private chart; therefore, if you want to create more charts, you have to delete the old charts to create more space for new ones.

You can also set up an offline plotly library with the following code:

```
import plotly.plotly as py
import plotly.graph_objs as go

# Offline plotly mode
from plotly.offline import init_notebook_mode, iplot
init_notebook_mode(connected=True)
```

You can easily create basic plotting techniques using Matplotlib, Pandas visualization, and the seaborn library. You can also learn how to use the various features to change your chart's color, grid, and scale. In the following sections, we will focus on using the Matplotlib package.

Plotting Simple Data with Matplotlib

Plotting a graph is very easy. We will look at an example of plotting your first line graph.

```python
import matplotlib.pyplot as pt



# x axis values

x = [1,4,5]

# y axis values

y = [2,3,1]



# plotting the points

pt.plot(x, y)
```

```python
# naming the x axis
pt.xlabel('x - axis')
# naming the y axis
pt.ylabel('y - axis')


# Enter graph title
pt.title('Welcome to the first graph!')


# function to show the plot
pt.show()
```

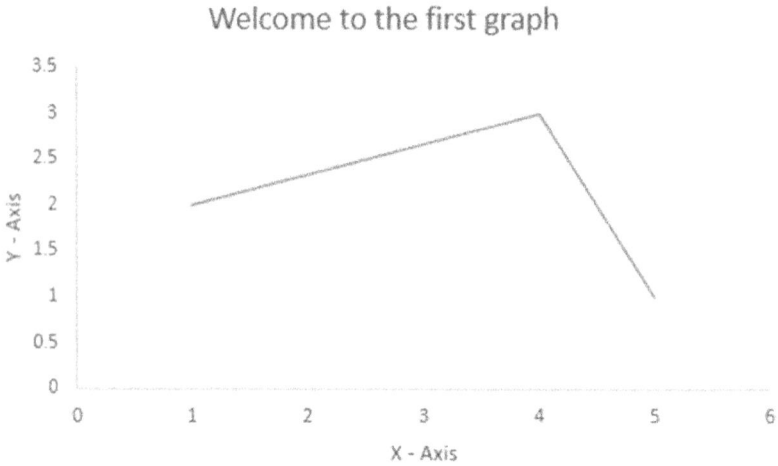
Welcome to the first graph

We use the `.plot()` function to plot the graph on the canvas.

You can use both the `.xlabel()` and `.ylabel()` functions to name your *x*- and *y*-axes.

The `.title()` function allows you to title the graph.

The `.show()` function displays the graph.

Customizing Your Plots

You can customize the graph to your needs, including the plotting point color, style, and sometimes even the scale.

116

```python
import matplotlib.pyplot as plt
#create x and y variables
x = [1,2,3,4,5,6]
y = [2,4,1,5,2,6]
  # plotting the points
plt.plot(x, y, color='green', linestyle='dashed', linewidth = 3,
          marker='o', markerfacecolor='blue', markersize=12)
 plt.ylim(1,7)
plt.xlim(1,7)
plt.xlabel('x - axis')
plt.ylabel('y - axis')
plt.title('Graph customization!')
  # show the plot
plt.show()
```

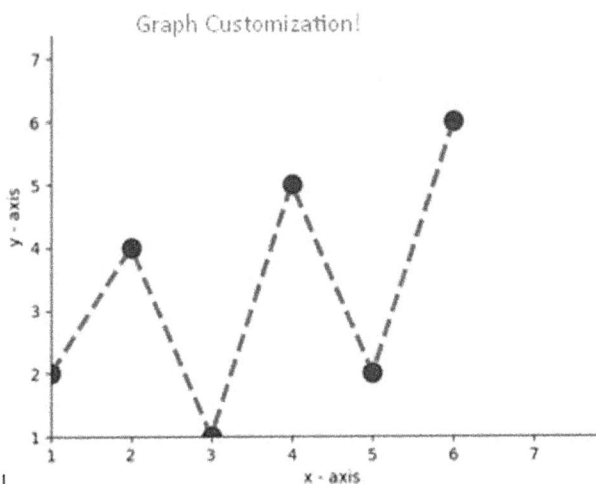

Adding a Background Grid to Your Plot

```
import plotly.plotly as py
import plotly.graph_objs as go
import plotly.tools as tls
import matplotlib.pyplot as plt
import numpy as np

grid = plt.grid()
x = np.linspace(0, 14, 100)
gflip= -1
for i in range(1, 6):
    plt.plot(x, np.sin(x + i * .5) * (6 - i) * gflip)

plotly_grid = tls.mpl_to_plotly(grid)
plotly_grid['layout']['x-axis']['showgrid'] = True
plotly_grid['layout']['y-axis']['showgrid'] = True

plotly_url = py.plot(plotly_grid, filename='background-grid')

plt.show()
```

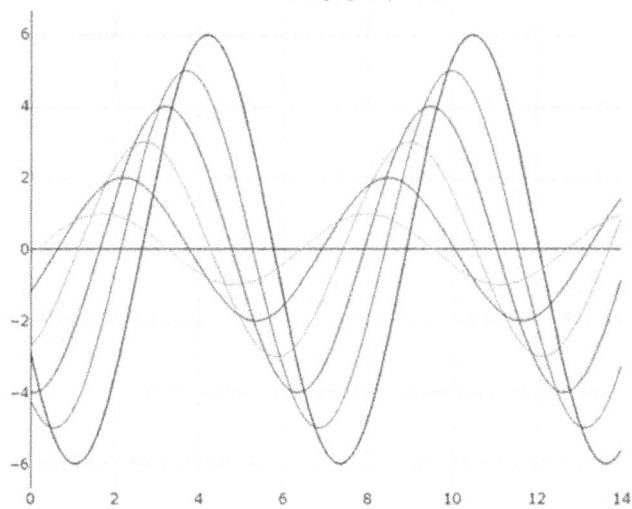
Changing Graph Grid

Changing Axis Label Font Size

```
import matplotlib.pyplot as plt
import numpy as np
import plotly.plotly as py
import plotly.tools as tls


mpl_grid = plt.grid()
label = mpl_grid.add_subplot(111)

t = np.arange(-5.0, 5.0, 0.01)
s = np.sin(4 * np.pi * np.absolute(t)) * np.exp(-5 *
np.absolute(t))
line, = label.plot(t, s, lw=2)

label.set_title("My plot title")
label.set_xlabel("X-Axis fontsize=18", fontsize=18)
label.set_ylabel("Y-Axis fontsize=16", fontsize=16)

plotly_grid = tls.mpl_to_plotly( mpl_grid )

plot_url = py.plot(plotly_grid, filename='mpl-axes-
font-size')
```

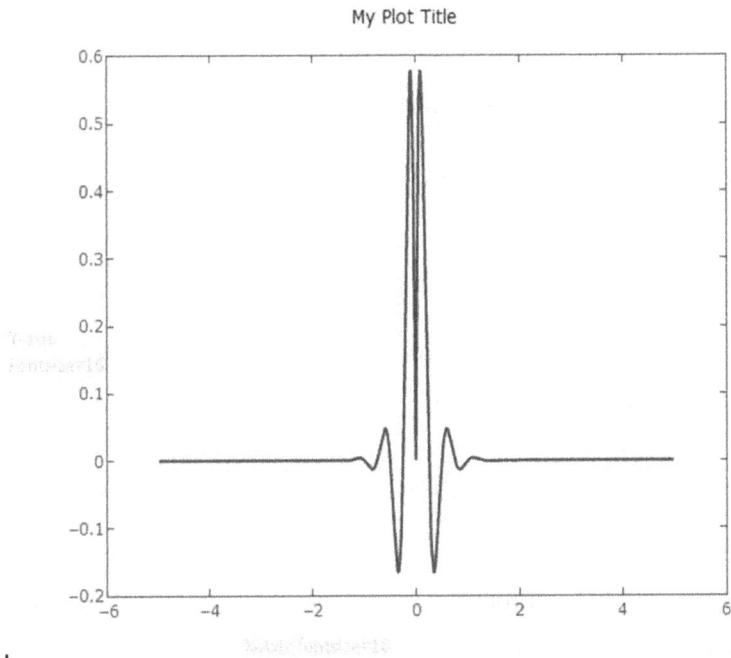

Visualizing Time Series Data

Time series data is a sequence of discrete-time data taken over successive, equally spaced points in time. A collective observation of sales data for one month represents a time series data. This time series data defines and consistently measures the sales revenues at successive, equally spaced points in time.

Time series data comprises three components:

- **The trend** (activities with long-term direction)

121

- **Seasonal** (systematic or calendar-related movements)

- **Irregular** (unsystematic or short-term fluctuations)

Time series can either be in the form of *stock* or *flow*. A **stock** series measures data attributes at a certain point in time, which investors would commonly view as "stocktales." For example, employee payroll data is a monthly stock measure that determines whether the employee has rights to any payments that month.

A **flow** series is a measure of activities that have taken place over a given time period. An example is the survey of manufacturing activity for a week. Every day, the company would produce a specific amount of products within a week; they can sum up the amounts to give a total value of production for that week.

Example

Time series data is a sequence of discrete-time data taken over successive, equally spaced points in time. A collective observation of sales data for one month represents a time series data. This time series data defines and consistently measures the sales revenues at successive, equally spaced points in time.

Time series data comprises three components:

- **The trend** (activities with long-term direction)

- **Seasonal** (systematic or calendar-related movements)
- **Irregular** (unsystematic or short-term fluctuations)

Time series can either be in the form of *stock* or *flow*. A **stock** series measures data attributes at a certain point in time, which investors commonly view as "stocktales." For example, employee payroll data is a monthly stock measure that determines whether the employee has rights to any payments that month.

A **flow** series is a measure of activities that have taken place over a given time period. An example is the survey of manufacturing activity for a week. Every day, the company would produce a specific amount of products within a week; they can sum up the amounts to give a total value of production for that week.

Example

In this example, I will use the shares value data, you can download a sample file to use from this link. This data shows the sales volume and closing stock prices of shares for a period of two years.

Visualizing this data will enable you to understand the shares trends and when shares value is high, low or even open prices. You need to analyze the trends before making any investment decision.

Timestamp	closing value	volume	open	high	low
12/20/2018	192.23	46541444	191.72	197.18	191.4501
12/13/2018	192.23	46725710	191.63	197.18	191.4501
12/12/2018	194.17	50991030	199	199.85	193.79
12/9/2018	204.47	34317760	205.55	206.01	202.25
11/8/2018	208.49	25289270	209.98	210.12	206.75
11/7/2018	209.95	33291640	205.97	210.06	204.13
11/6/2018	203.77	31774720	201.92	204.72	201.69
11/5/2018	201.59	66072170	204.3	204.39	198.17
11/2/2018	207.48	91046560	209.55	213.65	205.43
11/1/2018	222.22	52954070	219.05	222.36	216.81
10/31/2018	218.86	38016810	216.88	220.45	216.62
10/30/2018	213.3	36487930	211.15	215.18	209.27
10/29/2018	212.24	45713690	219.19	219.69	206.09
10/26/2018	216.3	47191700	215.9	220.19	212.67
10/25/2018	219.8	29027340	217.71	221.38	216.75
9/24/2018	215.09	39992120	222.6	224.23	214.54

From the shares_value data, we can plot a single column data

```python
import pandas as pd


# Read in data with two headers

data = pd.read_csv('shares_value.csv',
header=[0,1], index_col=0)



# Retrieve column data
```

```
sales = df.loc[:, ('timestamp', 'sales volume')]


# Plot the data in a chart

sales.plot()
```

Shares values

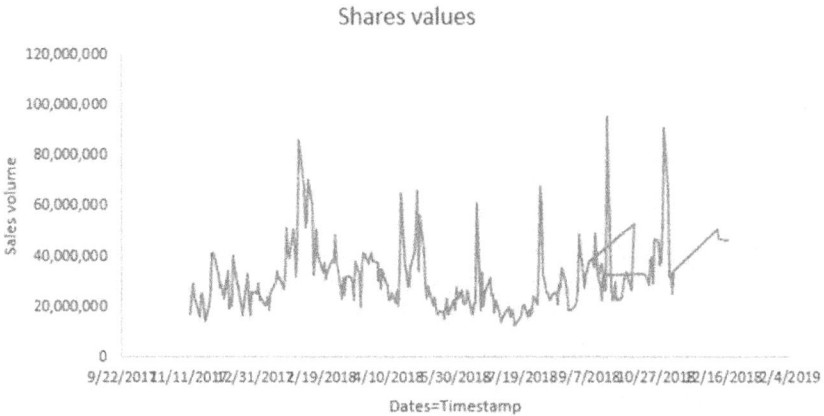

From the graph, notice that sales are always low at the beginning of the year but increase during the year, with high sales recorded at the end of the year. This represents an upward trend within the year, although there are months where sales are low.

Using a Scatter Matrix Data Visualization Tool

A **scatter plot** or **scatter matrix** is a collection of scatter plots organized to form a grid. The grid shows a relationship between a pair of variables where you would plot each variable against the other. For example, if you have k variables, your scatter matrix will have k rows and k columns.

A scatter plot is a powerful data visualization tool that conveys detailed information. The chart represents a two-dimension data visualization with dots generated from two variables. The program plots the data against the x- and y-axes.

For example, in a graph representing the **weight of children**, each dot will represent a **single child with his or her height**. The graph will measure the children's *height* along the x-axis, while representing the children's *weight* along the y-axis.

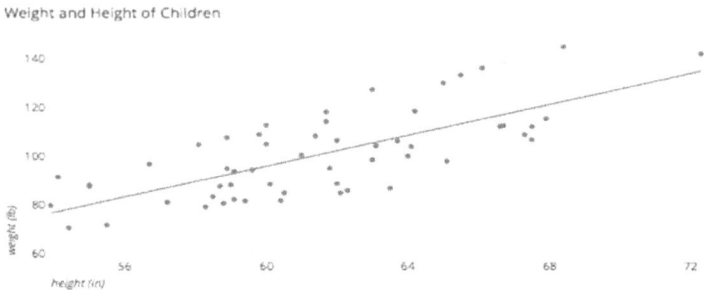

Weight and Height of Children

126

When to Use Scatter Charts

Scatter plots are useful when you want to show the relationship between two variables. They determine a **linear correlation** between different variables. In the above example, the chart not only shows the weights and heights of children but also visualizes the relationship between the weight and the height. As the height increases, so does the weight; therefore, we can say that height correlates to the weight of each child.

If there is no correlation between the variables, the chart will display the variables as scattered on the coordinate plane. In case of a large correlation, the dots will concentrate near the straight line.

If the y-axis variable *increases* as the x-axis variable *increases*, then the correlation is **positive**; if the y-axis variable *decreases* when the x-axis variable *increases*, it is a **negative** correlation.

If you can't tell whether y-axis is increasing or x-axis is increasing (and vice versa), then you have **zero correlation**.

A positive correlation has a maximum of +1 and 100% when the dots lie exactly along the straight line. A negative correlation has a maximum of -1 and 100%.

Types of Scatter Charts

There are three types of scatter diagrams based on the correlation.

- No Correlation

- Moderate Correlation

- Strong Correlation

Scatter Diagram with No Correlation

This scatter chart has a **zero correlation** because the dots are spread randomly and you can't draw any line between them. There is no relationship between the two variables.

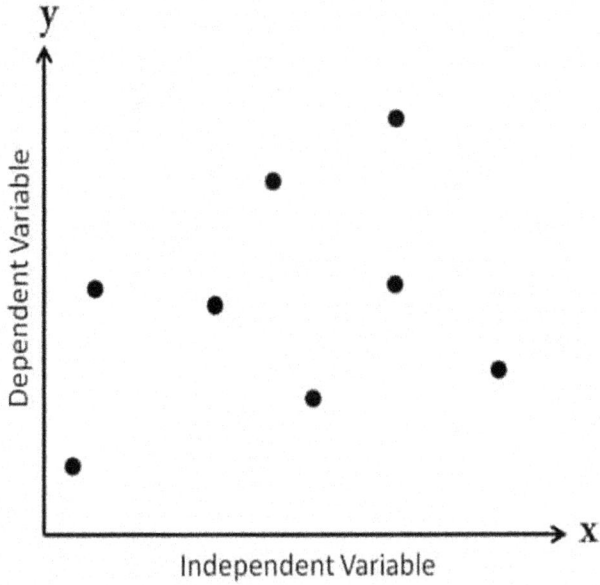

y

Dependent Variable

Independent Variable

X

Scatter Diagram with Moderate Correlation

We can also call this chart a scatter diagram with **low degree of correlation**.

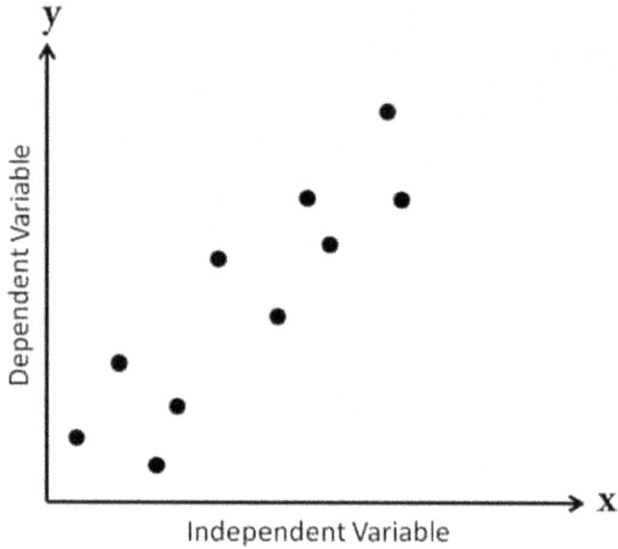

The data points in this chart somewhat close together, with some correlation between the two variables.

Scatter Diagram with Strong Correlation

This scatter plot has a high degree of correlation because the data points grouped close together. You can easily draw the line following the data points.

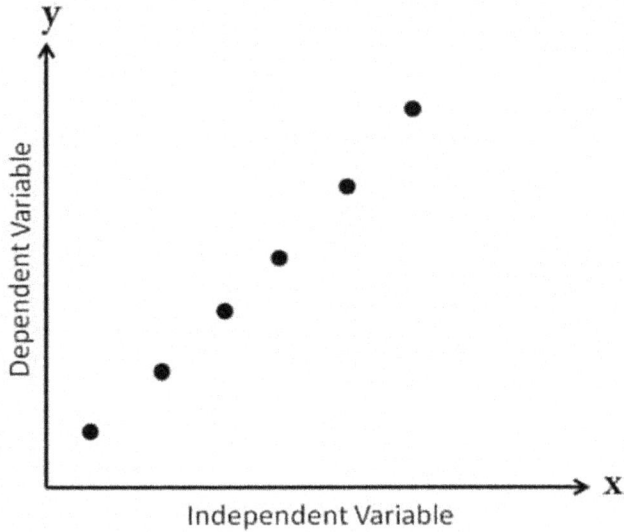

This scatter chart shows the variables as closely related to each other.

When drawing scatter plots, you can classify them based on the trend and the slope of the data points.

Advantages of Drawing Scatter Plots

- Plotting the chart is relatively easy.

- Observation and reading the plotted data is straightforward.

- It is the best tool to show you the relationship between two variables.

- The chart can easily show you non-linear data patterns.

- It shows the range of data flow; you can determine maximum and minimum data values.

How to Plot the Scatter Matrices

Here, we will create a **simple scatter plot** using matplotlib *scatter ()* method.

```
import matplotlib.pyplot as pt


# x-axis values

x = [2,3,4,5,4,5,7,8,10,12]

# y-axis values

y = [1,2,3,6,5,6,7,8,9,10]


# plotting points as a scatter plot
```

```python
pt.scatter(x, y, label= "series", color= "blue",
                marker= "bo", s=32)

pt.xlabel(' x - axis')

pt.ylabel(' y - axis')
# plot title
pt.title(' Scatter Diagram!')
pt.legend()

# function to show the plot
pt.show()
```

SCATTER DIAGRAM

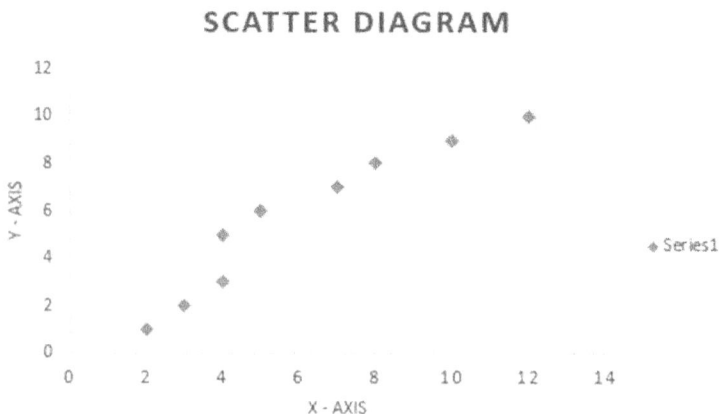

Scatter Matrix Using Pandas Library

Creating a scatter matrix will help to visualize data trends. Pandas library uses a Matplotlib package to display the scatter matrix.

When creating a scatter plot in Pandas library, call the *<dataset>.plot.scatter()* function and pass the arguments to the function (for the x-axis column and that for the y-axis column).

Example: Plotting Scatter Matrix Using Shares_value.csv Data

```
import matplotlib.pyplot as pt

import pandas as pd

from sklearn import datasets
```

```
%matplotlib inline



pt.style.use('style')

#load data to plot

data = pd.read_csv (shares_value.csv)

data = pd.DataFrame('Timestamp', 'open', 'low',
'high')

pd.scatter_matrix(data, alpha=0.2)

pt.show()
```

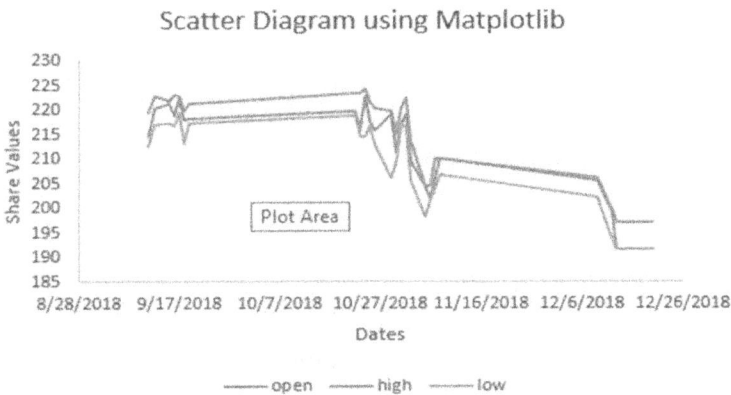

Scatter Diagram using Matplotlib

In the above graph, you learnt that there is a close correlation between low, open and high values daily. So you can use one of those values to determine trends in stock prices.

Chapter Summary

Data visualization is an essential tool for data presentation. It enables you to display data in a simple and easy-to-understand manner. Various data visualization tools like charts, graphs, and other representations of data in a summarized form. This helps to grasp information from mass volumes of data within a few minutes.

In this chapter, you learned how to visualize data using various tools, including visualizing time series data. You also learned how to plot data using Matplotlib package and data visualization using Pandas library.

We went over how to plot different charts including scatter matrices and how to change chart color, grid, and scale. In drawing scatter diagrams, we can now highlight the essentials for using scatter plots for data presentation and how you can read the data points to determine the relationship between two variables.

In the next chapter, you will learn about common financial analysis tools you can use to analyze your data for future decision-making.

A Short message from the Author:

Hey, are you enjoying the book? I'd love to hear your thoughts!

Many readers do not know how hard reviews are to come by, and how much they help an author.

I would be incredibly thankful if you could take just 60 seconds to write a brief review on Amazon on the product page, even if it's just a few sentences!

Thank you for taking the time to share your thoughts!

Your review will genuinely make a difference for me and help gain exposure for my work.

Common Financial Analysis

What is Financial Analysis?

Financial analysis is a process used to examine the financial data of an organization to make informed decisions. It is an assessment tool to determine how profitable a venture is in terms of its income statement, cash flow, and its financial position. Financial analysis on any project undertaken by the organization determines how viable it is and recommends the management team on areas they need to improve.

Many industries use Python in finance for qualitative and quantitative analysis. They also use Python in stock market analysis, prediction, and machine learning.

There are powerful libraries in Python like Pandas, Numpy, and Anaconda that organizations use for financial data analysis and other calculations. These libraries can easily integrate with other platforms and languages to perform specific functions.

The Pandas library plays a larger role in working with data. It helps to analyze large volumes of data and visualization, thus making it easy to perform statistical calculations.

Libraries like Scikit-Learn and PyBrain are useful in machine learning and prediction analysis.

Trading Financial Analysis

Traders require a lot of analysis in the stock market, and they commonly use Python to handle analysis more often than other programs. The program makes it easy for developers to define winning trading strategies and also gives some tips on stock trading patterns in the market.

Python development framework makes it easy to examine stock information in the stock exchange market and make an informed decision. Investors can also get some recommendations on open stock opportunities they can invest in based on the analyzed data.

Information like stock prices and current market prices is available to investors to make the right decisions on what to invest in and when. Stock prices change daily, which can affect the value of an investment, thus the need for carrying stock analysis and visualization.

Financial analysis of the stock trade enables you to measure your daily gains or losses especially if you have invested in long term stocks. These stocks act as a way of generating passive income since you will receive a share of profits from the company proceeds.

The goal of any trading financial analysis is to maximize returns for the investors despite stock constraints.

Some of these constraints include;

· Individual ethical concerns,

· Current income needs of an individual and,

· Risk involved

Stock prices change on a daily basis, therefore, there is a need to monitor the daily changes and calculate the daily returns based on your investment. Monitoring the daily changes will enable you to know the magnitude of change and predict the future changes in the stock prices.

Daily stock returns also helps in estimating your future total returns on all stock investment. It is important to determine daily return for each stock investment. Your future returns will be based on dividends paid and changes in the share price.

Share price changes can be in the form of change in per-share-earnings and change in the price-to-earning on multiple stocks.

Daily Returns

Analysing daily stock returns helps to monitor its rate or magnitude of change. It helps measure the dollar change in the stock price and it is expressed as a percentage of the previous day stock closing price.

If the return is positive, the stock price grows in value, whereas a negative return shows a loss in value. Stocks with higher daily returns are perilous compared to stocks with lower positive and negative daily returns.

To calculate your daily stock return, you need to compare the closing price of the previous day with the current stock price and express the difference between the prices into a percentage value.

You can calculate the daily return value manually or use an online calculator for quicker results. You can also develop a Python code that will automatically generate your daily return based on a few parameters.

How to Determine Daily Return

To know your daily return, you need to first know how much the stock is worth. To do this, visit financial websites that give daily stock price information. Search stock prices of the specific company you're interested in from the website search button.

Once you get the results, you can get the daily return by dividing the **current price** by the **previous day's closing stock price**, then multiply by 100.

Daily Return = [Current stock price/previous closing stock]*100

Assume the current closing stock is $2.25 and the previous closing stock was $25.5 then,

Return for the day =[$2.25/$25.5]*100 to get 8.8%

To calculate the gain or loss, subtract the **current stock price** from the **previous closing price**. Multiply the results by 100 to convert it to a percentage, then multiply by the **number of shares you owe**.

Actual gain/loss = [(Previous closing stock-Current stock price)*100]*shares

You can also convert your daily return to annual return. The return per day is expressed as a decimal number.

```
Daily investment return = [Amount of return / value of the
investment] *100
```

```
Annual return = [(Daily return+1)³⁶⁵ -1]*100
```

$$Annual\ return = [(Daily\ return+1)^{365} -1]*100$$

To convert our daily return to annual return, we raise the figure to the power of 365 (*days*), then subtract by 1. We can convert the value we get into percentage by multiplying with 100.

For example, if you have an investment that gives you 0.06% daily return, convert this figure into decimal format and convert the figure to annual returns using the formula:

$$Annual\ return= [(0.0006+1)^{365}-1]*100=24.5\%$$

Calculating Daily Return via Python Pandas.

To use Pandas library, you need to import all the modules to your Python library.

```
import Pandas as pd

import numpy as np

import matplotlib.pyplot as plt

import Pandas_datareader as web
```

After importing the modules, you can download historical prices of data from the Internet and use the downloaded prices to calculate the returns.

144

Example

In this example, we will download **stock data** that shows the stock performance for a certain period, then use those historical prices to perform the returns.

```
import pandas as pd

import numpy as np

import matplotlib.pyplot as pt

import pandas_datareader as web

from pandas_datareader import data as pdr

sp= web.get_data_yahoo("NFLX"),

start_sp= datetime.datetime ("2009/01/01"),

end_sp =datetime.datetime('2018/03/01'),



print(sp.head())
```

when you run the program, this is the output you will be able to obtain.

	High	Low	...	Volume	Adj Close
Date			...		
2009-01-02	4.357143	4.200000	...	6605200.0	4.267143
2009-01-05	4.562857	4.302857	...	13044500.0	4.562857
2009-01-06	4.750000	4.590000	...	12065900.0	4.705714
2009-01-07	4.734286	4.571429	...	10133900.0	4.672857
2009-01-08	4.797143	4.485714	...	8175300.0	4.735714

Stock Performance for the top 5 stocks

To obtain the **closing stock**, run this code:

```
sp['Adj Close'].plot()

#name the axis

pt.xlabel("Dates")

pt.ylabel("Adjusted closing price")

pt.title("Share prices data")

pt.show()
```

Calculating Daily Return

To calculate the daily return, we use pct_change() function

```
stock_daily_returns = sp['Adj
Close'].pct_change()



print (stock_daily_returns.head())
```

Output

```
    Daily Return Based on Adj Closing stock
Date              Adj Closing Stock
2009-01-02              NaN
2009-01-05        0.069300
2009-01-06        0.031309
2009-01-07       -0.006982
2009-01-08        0.013452
Name: Adj Close, dtype: float64
```

Insert daily return chart for stock price data:

```python
#Set the graph size and axis

fig = pt.figure()

pt = fig.add_axisrange([0.1,0.1,0.8,0.8])

pt.plot(stock_daily_returns)

pt.set_xlabel("Date")

pt.set_ylabel("Percent")

pt.set_title("Daily returns data")

pt.show()
```

Daily Returns Data

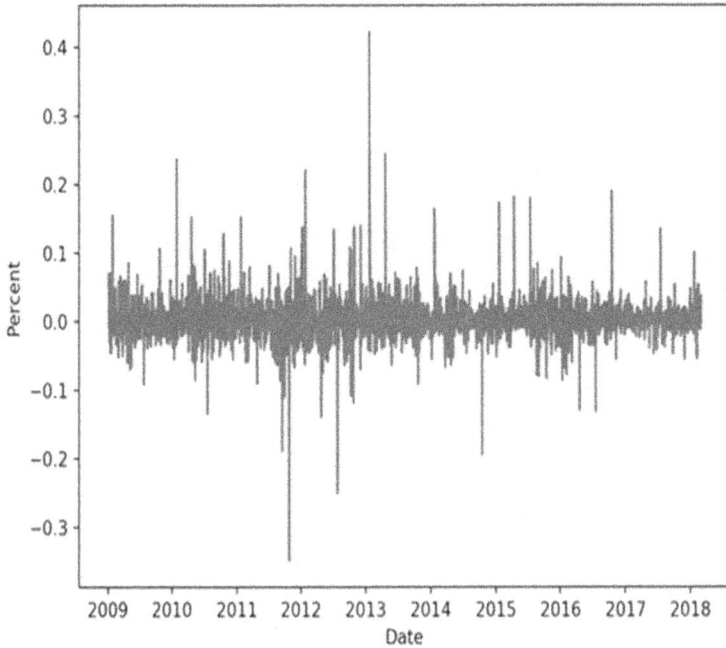

Cumulative Daily Rate of Return

You would use the cumulative return to show the total amount of
return an investor can receive from his or her investment, irrespective of
the time. It is the aggregate amount lost or gained in an investment
independent of the time involved. You would always express the
amount as a percentage.

Coming up with the daily returns will make it easy to plot the
volatility of the investment. If you have been investing in stocks for a

while, you can determine the growth of your investment by calculating cumulative returns.

To obtain the cumulative return in Python, use the *cumprod ()* function:

```
Sp_cum_returns = (Sp_daily_returns +
1).cumprod()
```

Using data from the previous example about daily returns, we can plot a **graph of daily cumulative returns**:

#prepare graph size

fig = pt.figure()

pt = fig.add_axisrange([0, 70])

sp_cum_returns.plot()

pt.set_xlabel("Date")

pt.set_ylabel(" Investment")

pt.set_title("Cumulative daily returns data")

pt.show()

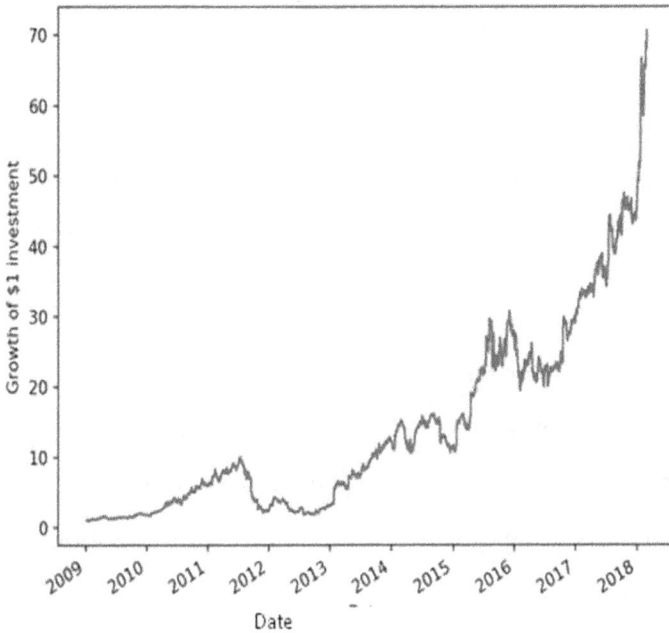

Cumulative daily returns data

Moving Window

In finance, we would call evaluating statistical trading metrics over a sliding window time frame as a moving window. A moving window means isolating subsets of a time-dependent measurement through taking the last *n* time segment and using each time segment as an input in deciding the best trading strategy. It analyzes price history by averaging the daily stock prices over time. Many investors and organizations use moving windows to determine moving averages of stock prices.

A moving window acts as a technical analysis tool that smoothes out share prices by filtering out *"noise"* from the short-term price fluctuations. The technique uses past share prices and can easily identify the changing trends in prices and also determine support and resistance levels.

Moving averages show the lag in the current market prices as compared to past prices. The lag is directly proportional to the period; the longer the time, the greater the lag. The length of the moving window depends on the trading objectives. Here, investors use short moving averages for short-term trading.

If the moving averages of stocks are rising, then the security is in the uptrend whereas if the moving averages are reducing, they're indicated by a downtrend.

Moving averages are fully customizable and an investor can choose which time-frame they want to use when creating the averages. When finding the best time frame to use, you need to experiment with different time periods and choose the time that fits your strategy.

A moving average trend creates a constantly updated price average through smoothing out the price trends.

How to Calculate Moving Window

The moving average forms the basis of **momentum-based trading strategy**. You can get the rolling mean over a window period. When using the `rolling()` method with a window of twenty days, you can obtain the moving average.

Example 1:

Using `rolling ()`

```
import pandas as pd

# change the adjusted closing prices to
adj_prices

adj_price = msft_data['Adj_Close']



# calculate the moving average

wdays=20
```

```
MA =
pd.series((data['adj_price'].rolling(window=wday
s).mean())

Data=data.join(MA)

# print the result

print(MA)
```

Example 2

To calculate the moving window for the last 100 windows (*days*), we need to find the **closing stock** and also the **average of each window's moving average**. We can plot the moving average against the windows using the Matplotlib.

Matplotlib will enable you to plot the moving average against the stock price chart.

We will import Apple stock prices from 2011 to 2017 and calculate the moving average:

#extract Stocks Price from the internet using the following codes:

import pandas as pd

import datetime

154

```
import pandas_datareader.data as web

from pandas import Series DataFrame


stock_start = datetime.datetime(2011, 1, 5)

stock_end = datetime.datetime(2017, 1, 5)


dframe = web.DataReader("AAPL", 'Apple', stock_start, stock_end)

dframe.tail()
```

From the above data, we can calculate the **moving average**:

```
#code to calculate moving average with moving window
%matplotlib inline
#import matplotlib to plot the graph
import matplotlib.pyplot as plt
from matplotlib import style

# set matplotlib size
import matplotlib as mpl
mpl.rc('plot', size=(9, 8))
mpl.__version__

# setting matplotlib style using seaborn library
style.use('ggplot')

# set rolling window to 100
close_ad=dframe['Adj Close']
nav=close_ad.rolling(window=100).mean()

label = plot.add_axes([0,20,40,60, 80, 100)
label.set_xlabel("Date")
label.set_ylabel("Window")
label.set_title(" Moving Average")
close_ad.plot(label='AAPL')
m-avg.plot(label='m-avg')
plt.legend()
```

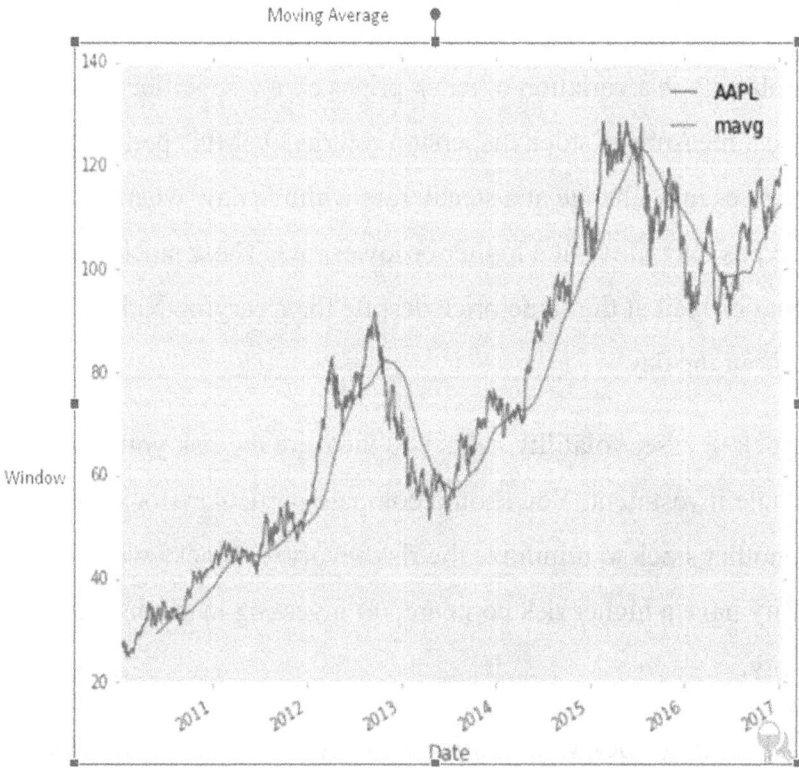

Moving Average

From this graph, you can see how the prices increase and decrease along the moving window.

Volatility Calculations

Volatility is a variation of stock prices over a specified period; a statistical measure of stock dispersion returns over this period. Some stock prices may change at a steady rate within a day, whereas other stock types may move at a higher or lower rate. These stocks may end up being offered at the same price despite their varying paths throughout the day.

Stock or asset volatility helps you measure the risk you're taking in any single investment. You should compare particular stock volatility with another stock to minimize the risk involved. Stocks with high volatility have a higher risk compared to investing in stocks with low volatility.

Calculating stock volatility is very easy, and it mostly depends on the size of the window (*number of days*). We would determine each stock volatility by the rolling-window standard deviation from the percentage change in the stock. The size of the stock window influences the overall results of the stock prices.

If the window is wider, there will be less representative of the stock measurement. When the window narrows, it makes it easy to obtain the standard deviation.

Example

If you want to invest in **Apple's stock securities**, you can first download **Apple's historical data** and use the data to determine the risk of your investment.

To calculate the volatility of your asset, you need to import the Numpy library.

```
import numpy as np

import matplotlib.pyplot as plt

# Define the minimum of periods to consider

min_periods = 75

# Calculate the volatility

vol = daily_pct_change.rolling(min_periods).std() * np.sqrt(min_periods)

# plot volatility

Vol.plot(figsize=(10,8))

Plt.show()
```

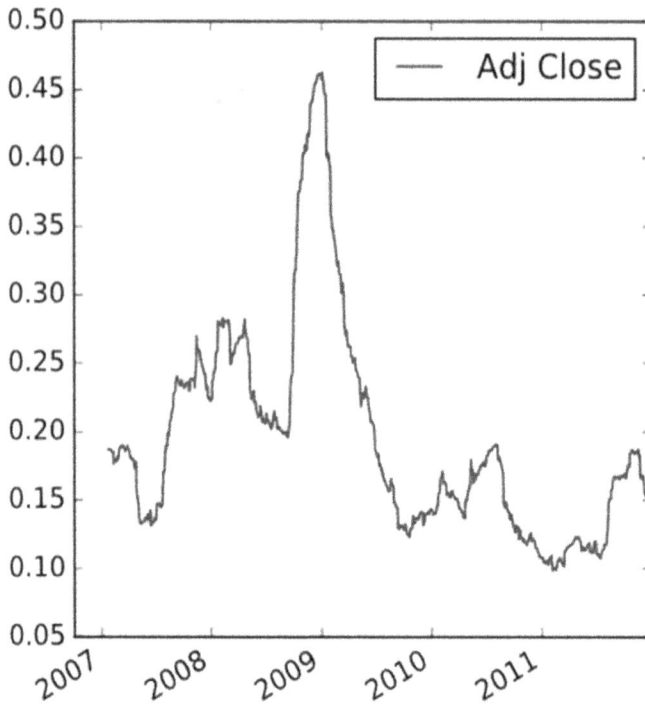

This example determines the volatility of a single investment (*Apple stock volatility*). If you need to compare the risk of investment in different stocks, you need to **diversify** your investment portfolio and carry out risk volatility for various stocks. Diversification also helps lower the volatility of an investment portfolio.

Dividends

Shareholders benefit from the wealth of the company by receiving dividends in the form of shares. Dividend payments encourage shareholders to continue investing in the company.

Companies give each shareholder additional shares; therefore, the shareholders can have healthy returns on their investments. The company doesn't have to part ways with its capital in the form of payout to the shareholders since they give the latter more shares instead of cash. Paying cash dividends reduces the company's value by the amount paid to the shareholders.

They issue dividends based on the number of shares each shareholder holds. For example, if the company issues dividends by 20%, each shareholder will have their stock holdings increase by 20%.

To calculate the dividend, you take the annual dividend and divide by the current stock price.

Dividend= Annual Dividend/Current Stock Price

For example, if Apple stock had share price of $50 and the annual dividend is $1.00 the dividend yield will be $0.02 or 2%.

You can use **dividend Assistant** tool to estimate your future dividend income. With the tool, you can link to your brokerage account or alternatively add all your stock holdings manually and track all your dividends.

dividend Assistant tool is a free dividend income management tool which can be used at any time. You can download it for free from www.dividend.com.

The table below shows the top rated dividend stocks from dividend.com with the stocks rated using the Dividend Advantage Rating System (DARS).

Stock Symbol	Company Name	DARS Rating	Ex-Div Date	Pay Date	Div Payout	Qualified Dividend?	Stock Price	Yield
MCR	MFS Charter Income Trust Shs Ben Int		2019-10-15	2019-10-31	0.06	Unknown	$8.36	8.67%
MGF	MFS Government Markets Income Trust Shs Ben Int		2019-10-15	2019-10-31	0.03	Unknown	$4.61	7.58%
CXE	MFS High Income Municipal Trust Sh Ben Int		2019-10-15	2019-10-31	0.02	Unknown	$5.45	4.51%
CMU	MFS High Yield Municipal Trust Sh Ben Int		2019-10-15	2019-10-31	0.02	Unknown	$4.67	4.63%
CIF	MFS Intermediate High Income Fund Sh Ben Int		2019-10-15	2019-10-31	0.02	Unknown	$2.59	9.44%

6. Ordinary Least Squares Regression

Ordinary least squares (OLS) regression is a statistical analysis technique used to determine the relationship between independent and

162

dependent variables. It measures the number of squares between the observed and predicted values of the dependent variable.

In the financial world, they often refer to this technique as the **linear regression model**. We use the OLS model to estimate, interpret, and visualize data on the squares.

We commonly use the statistical analysis tool **Statsmodel Python package** to perform linear regression. The package integrates well with Pandas and Numpy library to perform data analysis. Statsmodel has built-in tools for carrying out statistical testing and also checks how viable the set of plotting functions is.

Linear regression is one of the simplest modeling techniques, and it determines the relationship between the predictor variable (x) and its response (y). OLS operates with the assumption that the relationship takes the form of:

$$(y = \beta_0 + \beta_1 * x)$$

In the OLS estimator, the two β are used to minimize square distance between the values predicted and the actual values. This technique is common in linear regression since it is easy to understand the model and calculate coefficients.

Statsmodel package has several classes to modify OLS.

Example

Here, we will import data from the U.S. macroeconomic data from the website. In this case, we will load the **Longley dataset** into the Pandas DataFrame.

```
import numpy as np
import matplotlib.pyplot as plt
%matplotlib inline
import Pandas as pd
import statsmodels.api as sm
from statsmodels.iolib.summary2 import summary_col
from linearmodels.iv import IV2SLS


# extract longley dataset from the web with a column index 0
dframe =
pd.read_csv('http://vincentarelbundock.github.io/Rdatasets/csv/dat
asets/longley.csv', index_col=0)
dframe.head()# read the first five rows
```

Output

Longley Dataset from Web

GNP.deflator	GNP	Unemployed	Armed.Forces	Population	Year	Employed
83.0	234.289	235.6	159.0	107.608	1947	60.323
88.5	259.426	232.5	145.6	108.632	1948	61.122
88.2	258.054	368.2	161.6	109.773	1949	60.171
89.5	284.599	335.1	165.0	110.929	1950	61.187
96.2	328.975	209.9	309.9	112.075	1951	63.221

We can modify this example to determine the relationship between the **predictor** and the **response**.

We will use the **Gross National Product -"GNP"** as the **predictor** (*P*) and the variable **"employed"** as the **response** (*R*).

We can also add a constant term that will act as the intercept of the linear model.

```
R=df.Employed

P=df.GNP


#get the statsmodels.api library to add a constant term

P=sm.add_constant(X)


#print the output

P.head()
```

Output

Constant term,x

const	GNP
1	234.289
1	259.426
1	258.054
1	284.599
1	328.975

We can now perform regression analysis from the predictor and response by using the `sm.OLS class` and `OLS(R,P)` initialization method.

The `OLS(R,P)` function has two variables passed as array like object: *p* and *r*, where *p* can either be a Numpy array or Pandas DataFrame in form of *(n,m)*. The variable *n* will be the number of **data**

points while *m* will be the number of **predictors**. The response *r* will be either one-dimension Numpy array or the Pandas series of length *n*.

```
#call sm.OLS function (statsmodels.api library)

Estm=sm.OLS(R,P)
```

We also need to call OLS object `fit ()` method to fit our regression model. If your dataset has less than 20 samples, you will get a **Kurtosis test warning**. You may ignore the warning, as Kurtosis has a valid dataset up to 20.

```
Estm=sm.OLS(R,P)
estm = est.fit()


estm.summary()


C:/user/Faith/lib/Python3.6/dist-packages/scipy/stats/stats.py:127
6: UserWarning: kurtosistest only valid for n>=20
n=16


int(n))
```

Run the code to get the results.

OLS Regression Results

Dep. Variable:	Employed	R-squared:	0.967
Model:	OLS	Adj. R-squared:	0.965
Method:	Least Squares	F-statistic:	415.1
Date:	Sat, 08 Feb 2014	Prob (F-statistic):	8.36e-12
Time:	01:28:29	Log-Likelihood:	-14.904
No. Observations:	16	AIC:	33.81
Df Residuals:	14	BIC:	35.35
Df Model:	1		

	coef	std err	t	P>|t|	[95.0% Conf. Int.]	
const	51.8436	0.681	76.087	0.000	50.382	53.305
GNP	0.0348	0.002	20.374	0.000	0.031	0.038

Omnibus:	1.925	Durbin-Watson:	1.619
Prob(Omnibus):	0.382	Jarque-Bera (JB):	1.215
Skew:	0.664	Prob(JB):	0.545
Kurtosis:	2.759	Cond. No.	1.66e+03

R-Squared Linear Regression

Once you calculate the linear regression, you can determine how well the linear model fits the data using the **R-Squared model**. OLS minimizes the distance between the selected data points and the fitted line, reducing the sum of the squared residuals.

R-Squared, or the **coefficient of determination**, measures how close the program should fit the data to the regression line. That is, determine how scattered are the data points along the regression line. The program expresses it as a *percentage* (between 0 and 100%) of response variable variation results in the linear model.

It determines the relationship between the independent variables and the dependent variable. Once you come up with a linear regression model, you have to determine how well the data fits in the model. The regression model determines the difference between the observed values and the fitted values. That is, it finds the smallest sum in the squared variables in a dataset.

R-squared= Linear model variation/total variation

R-squared values are always between 0 to 100%. A 0% R-squared regression means that the model does not have any variability of the response data across its mean. The dependent variable mean is used to predict the dependent variable and the regression model. A 100% regression shows there is variability of the response data across its mean.

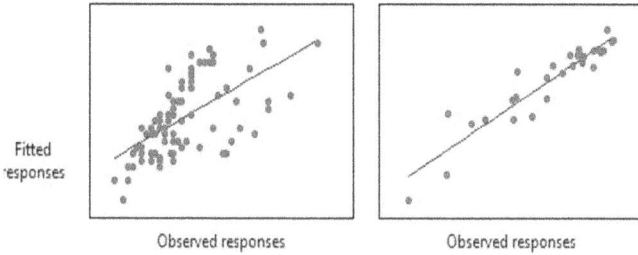

Plots of Observed Responses Versus Fitted Responses for Two Regression Models

Fitted responses

Observed responses   Observed responses

From the two plotted graphs, you will notice that the higher the R-Squared number, the better the model will fit your data. In this example, the graph on the left accounts for 38% variance, whereas the one on the right accounts for 87.4% variance. The higher the variance accounted for in the regression model, the closer the data points fitted in the regression line.

If the difference between the observed values and the predicted values are small then the regression model fits your dataset data. The fitted values should also be unbiased; they should be neither too high nor too low in the observation space.

When using R-Squared for data prediction, you may end up with a low R-Squared, indicating a good regression model or a high R-Squared value, the second which would not fit the data. Thus, R-Squared is not a good measure of showing whether a regression model is the best fit.

F-Statistic

F-statistic is a value returned when you do an **ANOVA test** or **regression analysis**. The test measures whether the variance between the two variables is different. The test uses f-distribution to indicate whether a group of variables are jointly significant and whether the hypothesis of the population variances are equal.

A variance is a measure of dispersion and shows how far the data scatter from the mean.

F-statistic is also referred to as f-test and it's mostly used to determine the overall linear regression value and provide the best fit to the line of regression. Compared to R-squared, f-test is more flexible and can be used in a wide variety of settings. It can also evaluate multiple data models and determine the best fit to the linear model.

F-statistic tests the equality of means and is the best variance analysis tool, especially when you want to accept or reject the **null hypothesis**. The null hypothesis is used to indicate that the model has no independent variables and fits the data well. If the independent variables in the model are not statistically significant, then the f-statistic will not be significant.

To determine whether a group of variables is equal, you can calculate the **F-statistic ratio**:

F-test= variation between sample means/variation with the samples

Chapter Summary

In this chapter, we learned how to carry out financial analysis and make the right decision when determining which financial securities to invest in. Some common financial analysis tools you should consider include:

- Calculating the daily return on each stock asset.

- Calculating the cumulative daily rate of return.

- Using moving windows to determine the volatility of a single investment.

- Calculating the number of dividends obtained from the profit proceeds of the company.

In the next chapter, you will learn about some common trading strategies you can use to maximize your profits and meet your financial needs.

Common Trading Strategies With Python

Building a Trading Strategy with Python

After you have successfully analyzed your data, the next step is to formulate a great trading strategy; something that will make you stand out from the rest and meet all your financial needs. There are some common types of trading strategies, which we will look at. You should read them carefully and understand them, so you can decide on which option will work best for you.

Common Trading Strategies

A **trading strategy** is the act of buying and selling of stock and securities on both a short-term and long-term basis, depending on their movements in the stock exchange chart. There are two main common trading strategies available: the **reversion strategy** and the **momentum strategy**.

Momentum Trading Strategy

We also know the **momentum strategy** as the **trend or divergence trading**. It is a technique in which investors rely on the recent price trend to buy and sell shares. Traders operate on the assumption that stock assets moving in a certain direction will continue to do so or follow that path until that trend loses its strength.

Entrepreneurs choose this strategy entirely based on the movement of a quantity from its current position. They believe that stocks move upwards or downwards, and with this, you can identify the direction of the momentum. The rate of a price change and trading volume affect momentum trading.

Momentum direction= Previous price- current price

There are two categories of the momentum strategy: **relative momentum** and **absolute momentum**.

Relative Momentum: This involves comparing the performance of different securities within the same asset class. The investor compares the assets against each other and buys the strong-performing security and sells the weak-performing security asset.

Absolute Momentum Trading: In this, the investor compares the current price of the security against the previous historical performance in the time series data.

Indicators of Momentum Strategy

Relative Strength Index (RSI): measures the strength of the current price trends. It shows how strong the current stock is in relation to previous stock performance. This information helps determine the time stocks are being overbought or oversold.

Rate of Change (ROC): shows the percentage change in price between the current price and the nth period of the past prices. It shows the general trend in prices and oversold and undersold securities.

Commodity Channel Index (CCI): shows the variation of the stock price based on the statistical mean. It compares asset prices against the moving average and the mean deviation of the normal price. It shows excess buying or selling when the reading is above 100 or below -100.

Moving Average Convergence/Divergence (MACD): shows the fast and slow-moving stock price average. It indicates the moving average trend lines by showing the price momentum and the price trend reversal points. If the lines are far apart, the momentum is strong; however, if they are close together, the momentum is slowing down and the price will slowly move towards reversal.

Stochastics: compares the current stock price with a certain range for over a specific period. If the range will be 20, then any reading below 20 will show an upward price momentum. If the stocks reach an overbought condition (*reading above 80*) then it will show downward price.

Examples of this strategy are inclusive of **turtle trading, moving average crossover**, and the **dual moving average crossover**.

Moving Average Crossover: occurs when the price of an asset shifts from one side of the moving average to the other. The crossover detects a change in momentum, and entrepreneurs use it as a basis for decision-making on whether to enter or exit the market.

Dual Moving Average Crossover: occurs when the short-term average changes to a long-term average. When this occurs, the momentum is shifting towards the side of the short-term average. When the short-term average rises above the long-term average, a buy signal raised. When the short-term average falls below the long-term average, a sell signal generates.

Turtle Trading: a popular strategy first introduced by Richard Dennis. The base behind this strategy is to buy stocks during their 20-day high or sell them on their 20-day low.

Reverse Trading Strategy

Reverse strategy, or **convergence trading**, involves a change in the price direction of a security. Reversal can either be *upside* or *downside*. If the price is in an uptrend direction, then the reversal will be *downside*; however, if the asset prices are on a downtrend, then the reversal will be *upside*.

We base the strategy on how the movement of quantities will reverse eventually. This occurs based on the overall direction of the price. Moving average and trend lines are major indicators in spotting reverse prices. For example, in the mean reversion strategy, we believe the stocks will return to their mean and you can deploy them once they deviate from the mean. This is practical.

A good reversal strategy should be able to show the changes in price direction either going up or going down. The strategy may occur in **intraday trading**, which happens more quickly, like within a day, a week or even within months.

Reversals are important to different investors. A long-term investor may not be interested in intraday reversal, even though they are watching the reversals on a daily or weekly basis. A day trader is more interested in price changes, and even a five-minute price reversal is very important.

Another good example to support this strategy, apart from the mean reverse strategy, is the use of **pairs trading mean reversion**, which is like the reversion strategy. In the mean reversion strategy, the stock returns to its mean. For pairs trading mean reversion, if the investor identifies two stocks to have a high correlation, the change in the price difference between these two stocks is used to signal the trading events if either of the stocks moves out of correlation with the other.

Based on this argument, if the correlation between the two stocks *decreases*, then the stock with the higher price should be in the **short position**; therefore, the investor needs to sell them. The stock with a higher price, in the long run, will return to the mean. The stock with a low price will be in a long position because its price will rise as the correlation returns to normal.

These two are the most common, but that does not mean that they are the only ones. The market has other strategies that you will come across once in a while. A good example of this is the **forecasting strategy** that tries to predict the value and direction of a stock. Another one is the **frequency trading strategy**, which makes use of the microstructure of the market.

In the next sections, we will now focus on helping you develop your own unique, valuable, and efficient trading strategy.

A Basic Trading Strategy

To formulate your trading strategy, begin with the basics of quantitative trading, which would be the moving average crossover. I will help you develop a simple trading strategy that will help maximize your investment. This strategy involves creating two different **simple moving averages (SMA)** with different periods, for example, 40 and 100 days. If you have a short moving average that exceeds the **long moving average**, then you should go for long-term investment, whereas if you have a long moving average that exceeds the short moving average, you should exit.

One thing to remember is that if you go long, then it means that your reasoning is that the stock will *rise* in price and you expect to sell at a higher price later (remember the buy signal). If you go short and sell your stock, then it means that you expect to buy it a lower price than that which you have sold it for and make a profit (sell signal).

This strategy is simple but might seem complex at first. We will, therefore, look at it step-by-step.

Step 1

Define two different time period windows: **short window** and **long window**. Afterward, set up two types of variables and assign each variable an integer data type. Make sure the integer assigned to the short-term window is shorter than the one assigned to the long-term window.

Step 2

Set up an empty signal DataFrame (*"signal"*) to help in calculating the buy and sell signals. Copy *"aapl"* index to enable you determine daily buying and selling signals of *"aapl data."*

Step 3

After this, the next step is to create a column in the empty *"signals"* DataFrame created in step two. Initialize the column and assign value [0.0] to all the rows in this column.

Step 4

Once you finished creating all the variables and assigning values to the rows of the column, create a set of short and long moving averages for both long and short time windows. Here, we will use the `rolling()` function to calculate the rolling window period.

Specify the window and the `min_period` as the arguments to the `rolling()` function. For example, we will the window to be `short_window` or `long_window`, and a `min_period` of 1, in which 1 will be the minimum number of observations in the window chosen.

After setting up the window, you need to calculate the mean average of both short and long windows. Later, you will need to calculate the rolling mean by calling the `Mean ()` function.

Step 5

After getting the mean average for both short and long windows, you have to create a **signal** that shows when the short moving average bypasses the long moving average. You can do this on the condition that the window period is greater than the shortest moving average window.

```
djsignals['short_mavg'][short_window:] >
djsignals['long_mavg'][short_window:]
```

If the condition tested is *true*, then the initialized values [0.0] in the *"signal"* column will be overwritten to [1.0]. Note that from step 3, your program will only create a signal when the condition is *false* and the values remain [0.0].

We will now create a program that will enable you to generate a **real trading strategy**.

```
#import the libraries
import numpy as np
import Pandas as pd

# Initializing variables for short and long window
short_window = 40
long_window = 100

# Initialize`dfsignals` DataFrame with `signal` column
dfsignals = pd.DataFrame(index=aapl.index)
dfsignals['signal'] = 0.0

# short window over short moving average
dfsignals['short_m-avg'] = aapl['Close'].rolling(window=short_window,
min_periods=1, center=False).mean()

# long moving average over long window
dfsignals['long_m-avg'] = aapl['Close'].rolling(window=long_window,
min_periods=1, center=False).mean()

# Trade signals
dfsignals['signal'][short_window:] = np.where(dfsignals['short_m-
avg'][short_window:]
                                        > dfsignals['long_m-
avg'][short_window:], 1.0, 0.0)

# trading orders
dfSignals['positions']=dfsignals['signal'].diff()

#results
Print(dfsignals)
```

Run the program and view the signals DataFrame to understand the trading strategy.

Next, we will write a code that will plot both **short** and **long moving averages** for buy and sell signals using the Matplotlib.

```
# Import `pyplot` module as `plt`
import matplotlib.pyplot as plt

# Initialize the plot figure
figure = plt.size()

# create a subplot and label y-axis
label = figure.add_subplot(111, ylabel='Price in $')

# plot yahoo closing price
aapl['Close'].plot(ax=label, color='r', lw=2.)

# Plot moving averages
dfsignals[['short_m-avg', 'long_m-avg']].plot(ax=label, lw=2.)

# Plot buy signals
label.plot(dfsignals.loc[dfsignals.positions == 1.0].index,
        dfsignals.short_m-avg[signals.positions == 1.0],
        '^', marketsize=10, color='n')

# Plot sell signals
label.plot(dfsignals.loc[dfsignals.positions == -1.0].index,
        dfsignals.short_m-avg[signals.positions == -1.0],
        'v', marketsize=10, color='l')

# Show the plot
plt.show()
```

Long and short moving averages using signals

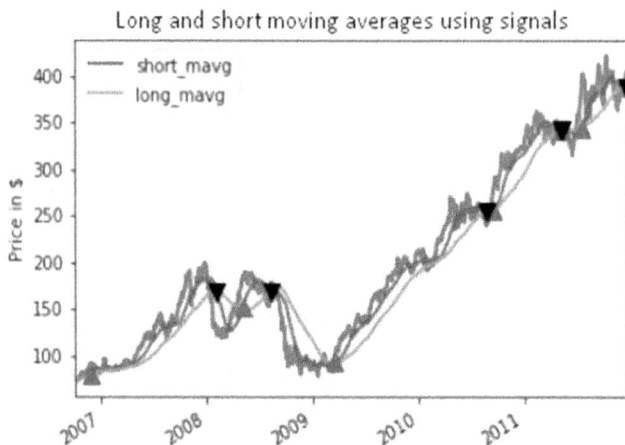

186

Evaluating Moving Average Crossover Strategy

Using the Pandas library, you can calculate the trading strategy metric and use the data to improve the strategy. To do this, use the **Sharpe ratio** to test whether the portfolio results are favorable and can help make smart investments.

The goal is to ensure that the investment returns are considerable and that the risks involved are manageable. When evaluating a portfolio, the greater the portfolio Sharpe ratio, the better the returns compared to the risks involved. If the ratio is greater than 1, then you can go ahead with that investment. If it's greater than 3, the investment is *excellent*.

Backtesting of Trading Strategies

Backtesting involves analysis of historical data to identify risks in any investment portfolio. It estimates the performance of any trading strategy chosen by the investor. That is, it estimates the strategy performance based on past data period.

It provides you with a step by step process in developing a trading strategy for a certain period of time. It guides you on how to approach any trading pattern and help you become a successful trader. For example, choosing a certain trading strategy may not work the way you expected and as a result, you may find yourself incurring losses. To avoid this, you can backtest your trading strategy to enable you to forecast how the strategy will perform in different market conditions.

To perform backtesting on any trading strategy or investment strategy, you need to have a detailed historical data. This is very important as it provides more information on synthetic data which is otherwise unavailable. With the historical data and all trades that occurred in the past, you can use rules defined by a specific strategy to determine the success of the investment portfolio.

Initially, large institution and professionals dealing with large volumes of data did backtesting but currently almost every investor is increasingly using it. Various web-based apps have emerged making the process easier.

Most investors operate with the assumption that what worked in the past is likely to work in the future and if a strategy worked poorly in the past, it will not work well in the future.

Advantages of backtesting

· Helps to optimize the performance of trading strategy.

· It is used to develop a successful trading system.

· Helps determine market conditions that has an impact on your profitability. It also provides you with real world statistics on profitability and risks involved.

· Helps you to easily adapt to a particular stock asset

· Provides you with realistic assessment on your capability and skills to successfully carry out a particular strategy.

Disadvantages of backtesting

· It is impossible to backtest strategies that affect historic prices

· When backtesting on a strategy, the chances that what worked in the past may work in the future are minimal.

· A lot of detailed historical data is required so as to get accurate results.

You can use backtesting to determine

·   Net gain or loss in an investment. Examining historical data for a period of time using a specific strategy rules will help determine the net profit or loss in an investment portfolio. It can also determine annual returns in an investment.

·   Used to determine volatility measure: backtesting is used as a tool to measure the maximum percentile in stock prices.

·   Determine moving average: It is used to draw the percentage gain or loss in an investment portfolio.

·   Capital exposure: In capital exposure, the percentage of the total capital invested in the market is determined. Using the capital invested, a win loss ratio chart is determined.

Factors to consider when backtesting a trading strategy

1.   Always consider pricing trends from a wide market in a given time frame for the strategy being tested. If a strategy was only backtested for two years, it will not give you accurate net gains. Therefore, the best backtesting results are the ones in which a strategy is backtested for a long-time period under different market conditions.

191

2.   Take into account into which market the backtesting was done. If backtesting of the wide market was done on financial institutions stocks, the same strategy will not work in tech stocks. It is a general rule that backtesting should be maintained on a particular genre of stocks.

3.   When developing the trading system, volatility measures are very important. This helps investors in making the right decision. For example, if the equity margin drops below a certain percentage, investors should keep the volatility low so as to minimize the risk.

4.   Having an increased exposure can help have higher gains in profits or higher losses. Less exposure will reduce the amount of profits or losses gained from an investment. At all times, you should keep the rate of exposure to below 70% so as to reduce risk as well as make it easier to transition into or out of any given stock asset.

5.   Using backtesting tools to determine the average gain or loss as well as determining the win-loss ratio can be essential in determining the optimal stock position. Investors can increase the average gains and win-loss ratio by taking on larger positions.

How to backtest trading strategy

Tools needed;

·   Historical data of the asset class you want to trade on

·   Trading simulation software

·   Strategy definitions and rules

·   Time period or number of days to perform backtesting

·   A detailed analysis of the backtest on previously backtested strategy.

Backtesting can be done automatically or manually. Automated backtesting are ultimate programs designed to open, manage, and close trades for you. Automated backtesting use trading simulators or softwares which visualize historical data and provide detailed stock performance on a step-by-step basis. You can easily buy the program from the market and use it to analyze stock strategies. In manual backtesting, you have to scroll through the trading chart in the trading platform and see how the strategy will perform and areas which needs some improvement.

From the detailed information provided, you can determine whether the trading strategy will be profitable based on its performance. It also helps you to spot market conditions which can affect the performance of the strategy and how they will affect the strategy in future. From this information, you can make your decision whether a particular trading strategy is good or not.

Trading simulation software

There are various quality backtesting software online. These are the top 6 backtesting software you can use to test your trading strategy.

1.   MetaStock: This is one of the most powerful tools for traders who want a powerful backtesting and forecasting tool. It provides excellent Win/Loss report.

2.   Quantshare: This tool is suitable for those who want to develop a detailed quantitative analytical system for multiple trading strategies.

3.   TradingView: This software is great for beginners. It has inbuilt strategies and a simple sleek interface to help traders write simple code to develop a strategy.

4.   TrendSpider: Provides a cutting edge for AI, has multiple timeframes for Auto Trendline recognition and provides system backtesting.

5.   Interactive Brokers: This tool is great for IB traders. It allows traders to develop a powerful portfolio strategy and testing with no programming knowledge.

Tradestation: Provides technical backtesting procedures for all Tradestation brokers. The tool integrates with Algorithmic Trading to provide the best backtesting.

Chapter Summary

In this chapter, we learned in-depth about common basic trading strategies using Python. We also learned how to use the momentum strategy and reverse trading strategy to compare investments from different companies and make the right investment decisions.

We went over how to forecast trends for existing market prices and compare them to the current market price. Along with that, you should also be able to calculate the number of dividends received from your investment in a company.

From backtesting subtopic, you're able to learn what is backtesting and why it is important to backtest a trading strategy before investing your capital in that strategy. You're also able to know the requirements needed and how to backtest.

Conclusion

Python is one of the best high-level programming languages for carrying out data analysis, machine learning, and creating web-based applications. There are other high-level programming languages in the market, but Python remains one of the best general-purpose programming languages. Over recent years, financial institutions have increasingly been using Python for all their financial needs.

Python is a great tool for data analysis and visualization, which is an important tool for financial analysis. The Python library is rich in tools and packages for performing statistical data and mathematical calculations. You can easily integrate Python with third-party apps and build a competitive structure for your organization to address all the consumer needs.

This tutorial on basic Python in finance will provide you with the basic knowledge for relying on Python programming language and understanding your financial market. It also showed you how you can use Python to make the right investment decisions.

If you want to dive into an investment in various financial securities, this tutorial should guide you on various trading strategies and how to choose the best trading strategy. You will also learn the key principles for successful trading and how to use time series data to predict financial security trends. If you plan to do all this yourself, this book hopefully has given you the guidance for getting started and setting up your workspace to observe current market trends.

After setting up the workspace, we imported the Python Pandas library to help in data manipulation. This book provided various ways you can import data from various sources into the Pandas development framework and manipulate it. You also learned how to use Excel to manipulate data and how to integrate Excel with Python.

You can now use the *Pandas_datareader()* function to import data from an Excel file and know how to read time series data in Python. You also learned how to rely on the predicted stock trends to make your investment decisions.

When dealing with large volumes of data, you need to bring forth data analysis and visualization tools to help interpret the data presented. Data visualization is a presentation of data in an easy-to-understand format using tools like graphs, charts, and scatter matrices. Data analysts rely on these tools to present data in simple formats.

You learned how to visualize time series data using Pandas library and plot data for an easy read. You can now plot different versions of time series data and customize your charts by changing color, font size, and grid. You also learned how to use scatter matrices to plot data points and read the relationship that exists between the plotted variables.

Financial analysis information is important to shareholders as they rely on this information when decision-making. Finance statements help to determine the financial strength and weaknesses of any investment. In our financial analysis chapter, we reviewed how to use the observed data to calculate daily returns, the cumulative daily rate of returns and how to calculate dividends and volatility.

Calculating the moving average will enable you to determine whether it is worthwhile to invest in a particular financial security or not. You can calculate the trading strategy metric and use the data collected to improve the strategy. I hope you learned much from this book and can now use Python in finance with confidence.

The end... almost!

Reviews are not easy to come by.

As an independent author with a tiny marketing budget, I rely on readers, like you, to leave a short review on Amazon.

Even if it's just a sentence or two!

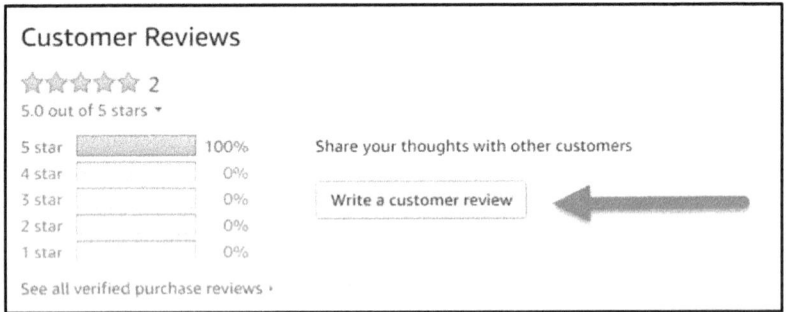

Customer Reviews

⭐⭐⭐⭐⭐ 2

5.0 out of 5 stars ▾

5 star	▰▰▰▰▰	100%
4 star		0%
3 star		0%
2 star		0%
1 star		0%

See all verified purchase reviews ›

Share your thoughts with other customers

Write a customer review

So if you enjoyed the book, please leave a review on the Amazon page.

I am very appreciative for your review as it truly makes a difference.

Thank you from the bottom of my heart for purchasing this book and reading it to the end.

References

Bowne-Anderson, H. (2018). Time series analysis tutorial with Python. *DataCamp*. Retrieved from https://www.datacamp.com/community/tutorials/time-series-analysis-tutorial

Data Analysis and Visualization with Python. (n.d.). *Geeks for Geeks*. Retrieved from https://www.geeksforgeeks.org/data-analysis-visualization-python/

Kumar, N. (n.d.). Graph plotting in Python: Set 1. *Geeks for Geeks*. Retrieved from https://www.geeksforgeeks.org/graph-plotting-in-python-set-1/

pandas.DataFrame.resample. (n.d.). *pandas 0.25.1 documentation*. Retrieved from https://pandas.pydata.org/pandas-docs/stable/reference/api/pandas.DataFrame.resample.html

Scipy Lecture Notes. (n.d.). Retrieved from http://scipy-lectures.org/

What is Momentum Trading? (n.d.). *FXCM*. Retrieved from https://www.fxcm.com/za/insights/what-is-momentum-trading/

Willems, K. (2019). Python for finance: Algorithmic trading. *DataCamp*. Retrieved from https://www.datacamp.com/community/tutorials/finance-python-trading

www.ingramcontent.com/pod-product-compliance
Lightning Source LLC
Chambersburg PA
CBHW071211210326
41597CB00016B/1769